# Confident French

from

A to Z

*Le basilic – La basilique ?*

# A Dictionary of Niceties and Pitfalls

by

Michaël Abecassis

the University of Oxford

PHÆTON
PUBLISHING LTD.
Dublin

# Confident French

FIRST PUBLISHED IN IRELAND & U.K. 2018
by Phaeton Publishing Limited, Dublin



Printed and bound in U.K. and in U.S.A.
second impression 2019

*British Library Cataloguing In Publication Data: a catalogue record for this book is available from the British Library*

ISBN: 978-1-908420-18-3 PAPERBACK
ISBN: 978-1-908420-19-0 HARDBACK

# PREFACE

This is not a grammar book, but a collection of language difficulties encountered by students at all stages of French study at the University of Oxford. Even after they have consulted several dictionaries and grammars of French—whether French, English, or bilingual—many students' questions remain unanswered, or hidden within a vast amount of information, or only partially dealt with by the reference books. The growing number of language forums on the internet is certainly an excellent thing, and is proof of the keen interest which the French language arouses in speakers and learners, but can we really trust the comments of web users who, from one website to another, and even sometimes within the same forum, may give contradictory explanations?

Here, we seek to give an account of language based on actual usage, while also remaining sensitive to language variation and change.

Entries are ordered alphabetically, and each is accompanied by examples, using quotations from authors or from everyday French.

The book is aimed at secondary school pupils, university students of French, and teachers of French, who, for either work or pleasure, have an interest in linguistic difficulties. While the work is far from exhaustive, it aims to encourage the reader to reflect on such issues.

The idea for this project came following the correspondence that we maintained for years with Réal St Jacques. He provided invaluable assistance at every stage of this work. We would also like to thank all of the students who, over several years, motivated us by the perceptiveness of their questions: without them the book would not have seen the light of day. Many of them, as well as several colleagues, helped in this project. We are particularly grateful to Wendy Anderson, Marcelline Block, Sophie Bocksberger, Robyn Boosey, Meriel Cordier, Katharine Handel, Célia Hoffstetter, Patrick Moran, Jade Patterson, Anne Salomon, and Louis de Saussure for their advice and support: the book has been greatly improved by their comments. Without their input, this research would not have come to fruition.

Michaël Abecassis, 2018

# INDEX OF TOPICS

Topics not listed above (e.g. 'article', 'passive', etc.) appear in alphabetical order within the text.

## À

The preposition *à* is not ordinarily found between two nouns, except in fixed expressions like *une bête à bon dieu* ('a ladybird'). We say *la maison de Pierre* rather than *la maison à Pierre. La barbe de papa* is literally 'daddy's beard', and not to be confused with the fixed expression *la barbe à papa* ('candy floss').

What is the difference between *une tarte au bleuet /aux bleuets* ?[1]

—*Une tarte au bleuet* gives more the idea of the taste (whether artificial or not), whereas *une tarte aux bleuets /aux fraises /aux framboises* places the emphasis more on the fruits which can be seen. We say *une tarte au citron* and *une soupe à la tomate* : the fruit is not seen, only tasted.

## ABÎME

*Elle avait l'impression après deux années au chômage d'être au fond de l'abîme.*[2]

Written with a circumflex, as the mnemonic sentence « *le chapeau de cime est tombé dans l'abîme* » reminds us.

It should not be confused with *une mise en abyme :*

*Par un processus de mise en abyme, le dramaturge insiste sur le ridicule de la société humaine.*[3]

The expression *mise en abyme* (also spelled *mise en abîme*) appears in verbal form in André Gide's *Journal* in 1893: *J'aime assez qu'en une œuvre d'art on retrouve ainsi transposé, à l'échelle des personnages, le sujet même de cette œuvre. … c'est la comparaison avec ce procédé du blason qui consiste, dans le premier, à en mettre un second « en abyme ».*

GIDE

1. The *bleuet* is a flower in France (cornflower), and a small blue fruit in Canada (blueberry).
2. After two years of being unemployed, she felt she had sunk into the depths of despair.
3. The playwright emphasises the absurdity of mankind through his use of *mise en abyme* ('play within a play').

*Abyme* and *abysse* have the same Greek root: etymologically, *abyme* comes from the Greek ἄβυσσος (*abyssos*), formed from the privative prefix α + βυσσός ('the seabed'), and containing a sense of the infinite. Since the 1990 reform of the Académie, *abime* without circumflex is acceptable.

## ACCENT

There is no rule of thumb regarding accent placement in French. However, in case of doubt, we recommend using syllabication to determine whether an '*e*' should bear an accent or not:

(a) If the '*e*' is NOT at the end of a syllable, then it is more likely to have no accent. Example: *cer/ti/fi/cat, let/trage*. In particular, in an '*ex*' or '*es*' sequence, the '*e*' has no accent: *Espagne, essentiel, esthétique, exemple, mesquin, textile* etc.

(b) If the '*e*' IS at the end of syllable, then it is more likely to have an acute accent. Example: *é/lé/men/taire* ; *dé/ter/mi/ner.*

(c) If a mute '*e*' comes after the '*e*', then it is more likely to have a grave accent. Example: *siècle, mètre.* Note, for instance, that there is a grave accent in *règle* (because the second '*e*' is mute) but an acute accent in *ré/gle/ment* (because the first '*e*' is at the end of a syllable and the second '*e*' is not mute).

In any case, pronunciation remains the best indicator. In the word *re/tour/ner*, for instance, the first '*e*' does not bear an acute accent, even though it is at the end of a syllable, because it is pronounced [ø]. However, there is an accent in the prefix *re-* when it is followed by a vowel (*réitérer, réarranger* etc.)

The circumflex often marks the dropping of an '*s*' which existed in the corresponding Latin word, e.g. *bête* (cf. English *beast*); *hôpital* (cf. English *hospital*). See also CIRCUMFLEX.

## ACHETER / S'ACHETER

Compare *elle a acheté une voiture /elle s'est acheté une voiture.*

*Acheter quelque chose* – i.e. the thing in question may be for oneself or for someone else; simply, the subject has made a purchase.

*S'acheter quelque chose* – i.e. the thing in question is bought for oneself. In using *s'acheter*, there is often an idea of 'taking pleasure in' or 'allowing oneself' something.

## ADÉQUAT

*J'espère que nous allons trouver l'équipement adéquat pour effectuer cet enregistrement audio.*[4]

The feminine form is *adéquate* /adekwat/.

## ADJECTIVE PLACEMENT

Why write *'un chat noir'* and not *'un noir chat'* ?

—The general rule in French is to place the adjective after the noun. When the adjective precedes the noun, it has a different meaning or it is for stylistic reasons: *une brave femme* (good, who is a good mother, etc.); *une femme brave* (who confronts danger with courage). *Un noir chat* would signify 'the black of the cat', which means nothing. *Un bleu ciel* is the blue which is that of the sky, that is, a certain shade of blue.

UNE FEMME BRAVE

## ADJECTIVES OF COLOUR

Colour adjectives used singly follow the normal practice of agreement for gender and number with the noun they qualify.

*De jolies fleurs bleues recouvraient la terre.*[5]– *Bleues* here agrees with *fleurs.*

Compound colour adjectives:

When two colour adjectives are combined, neither agrees with the noun. In most cases, the two adjectives are connected by a hyphen, although this is not obligatory: *des voitures bleu clair.*

Colour adjectives derived from nouns:

4. I hope we are going to find the right equipment to make this audio recording.
5. Pretty blue flowers covered the ground.

When a common noun is used as a colour adjective, it does not agree with the noun. In such cases, the noun *couleur* is generally understood: *des couvertures citron* (= *de couleur citron*) ; *des costumes kaki* (= *de couleur kaki*).

*Marron* and *orange* do not agree with the noun: *des yeux marron* ; *des coussins orange.*

*Amarante, écarlate, fauve, incarnat, mauve, pourpre* and *rose* are the seven exceptions. Considered as true adjectives, they *do* agree with the noun. For example, here *rose* agrees in gender and number: *des panthères roses.*

See also HYPHEN.

## AFFRES

*Ne souhaitant pas subir les affres cruelles de cette piètre existence, il décida de s'établir en Italie.*[6]

Feminine noun, and used always in the plural.

## AIL

*On trouve sur les marchés de Provence des aulx fraîchement cueillis qui sentent bon le terroir.*[7]

The plural form *aulx* (a homophone of *eau*) is rare (found particularly in the context of markets and trade) and tends to be replaced by *ails.*

## AIMER

*J'aime qu'elle soit à l'heure.*

*Je n'aime pas que tu sois en retard.*

Takes the subjunctive when it is used in the negative *and* the affirmative.

6. To escape from the torment of his paltry existence, he decided to settle in Italy.

7. Freshly picked garlic with a strong earthy scent can be found in the markets of Provence.

## ALLER

*Elle est allée / s'en est allée à Paris.*

In the first construction, the speaker is not concerned with the start location. The second construction contains an idea of moving 'from here to another place.' *S'en aller* is rare in the past and is typical of a higher register. In the present or future, it is quite frequent (*je m'en vais, elle s'en ira, ils vont s'en aller, va-t'en…*).

ALLER + present participle:

*L'effet de la crise va croissant.*

*Nous nous en allions, suant sur le sentier d'une colline escarpée.*[8]

The present participle following the verb *aller* (or *s'en aller*)[9] expresses an idea of continuity and progression. The use of the present participle preceded by the pronoun *en* emphasizes the consequence: *Les affaires allaient en s'améliorant.*

The usages of the gerund without *en* are rare and more literary.

PROUST

## AMARANTE

Colour adjective derived from a noun, but one which is an exception to the rule and therefore agrees normally:

*Le sol était jonché de feuilles de couleur amarante.*[10]

See ÉCARLATE, FAUVE, INCARNAT, MAUVE, POURPRE, and ROSE.

8. We struggled along the path up a steep hill.
9. It should be noted that the forms *je vas, je m'en vas* come from formal French up until the 19th century (*Le Bon Usage*, Grevisse et Goosse, 1993, §803, p.1209). It later slid toward the vernacular like the pronunciation of « *ouais* » in words ending in *–ois* or *-oi*. Many authors still use it as a vernacular form at the beginning of the 20th century (*Je vas seulement voir si mon feu ne s'éteint pas* —Proust, *Du côté de chez Swann*, 1913). *Je vas* is still occasionally heard in Quebec. On the function of *en* in *s'en aller* and how it has become fixed, cf. *Le Bon Usage*, Grevisse et Goosse, §656b, p.1003-4.
10. The ground was strewn with amaranthine [purple] leaves.

## AMBIGU / AMBIGUË

*Cette définition est ambiguë.*

The diaeresis is placed on the '*e*' rather than on the '*u*' of *ambiguë* for reasons of euphony and to show that the '*u*' is not silent, as it would be pronounced otherwise as */ambig/* (with *–gue* forming a syllable with a mute '*e*' and a hard '*g*'). Traditional practice is to place the diaeresis on the second letter to separate it from the first.

## AMBIGUÏTÉ

*Finissons-en avec ces ambiguïtés.*

The diaeresis enables the reader to differentiate the vowel '*u*' from the semi-consonant (as in *lui, nuit…*).

## AMENER / EMMENER

*J'ai amené ma sœur à la gare. Elle fut emmenée de force en prison.*

The prefix in *amener* (*ad* in Latin) means 'towards'. We use *amener* for taking someone to the park, etc.

The prefix in *emmener* (*in* in Latin which became *en* in Old French) means 'on, in, inside': '*emmener quelqu'un*' means to take someone from the place we are to another place:
*Quand il est parti, il a emmené sa fille* [i.e. 'he took her with him' ('to another place' is implied)].

This depends upon my position as enunciator: if the movement is made *toward me*, I use *amener*. If the movement is made *towards the exterior*, the referent distances himself /herself from me, I use *emmener*. For example: a teacher will say to her students « *N'oubliez pas d'amener vos affaires demain* » ('Don't forget to bring your belongings tomorrow'). This is about a movement of belongings towards the school, that is to say, the site where the enunciator is located. Whereas a father will say to his son « *Demain, c'est moi qui t'emmène à l'école* » ('Tomorrow, I am taking you to school'). Here, the movement is of the son toward the school, in other words, a site other than where the enunciator is located.

The same distinction applies to *apporter* ('take [someone /something] somewhere') and *emporter* ('take [someone/ something] with one').

## AMIANTE

*L'amiante est dangereux pour la santé.*

*Amiante* ('asbestos') is a masculine noun.

## AMOUR

*Cupidon le dieu de l'amour a décoché sa flèche pour lui percer le cœur.*[11]
*Ils regrettent plus que tout leurs amours perdues.*[12]

*Amour* is masculine in the singular and feminine in the plural. *Amour* was feminine in Old French. In the singular, however, it is now used as a masculine noun, with reference to *le Dieu Amour*. See also DÉLICE and ORGUE.

## ANAGRAMME

*Voilà une astucieuse anagramme.* – Feminine noun.

## ANANAS

*Rien de plus désaltérant qu'un bon jus d'ananas bien frais.*[13]

Masculine noun: *un ananas*. The pronunciation of '*–s*' is variable, although by convention the final '*–s*' is not pronounced in France. In Quebec, on the other hand, it is pronounced. The '*–s*' is a consequence of the Spanish origins of the word.

## AOÛT

*C'est au mois d'août qu'il se ressource dans sa maison de campagne.*[14]

AUGUSTUS

The word *août* comes from the Latin *augustus*. The pronunciation /ou/ is the one prescribed, but in common usage the final '*t*' is pronounced.

The pronunciation /aou/ is archaic. The *office de langue française du Québec* accepts as standard both /ou/ and /out/. The media in France has contributed to the popularisation of the form /out/.

11. Cupid, the god of love, shot his arrow to pierce [his/her] heart.
12. They regret their lost loves more than anything.
13. Nothing quenches your thirst better than delicious fresh pineapple juice.
14. In August, his house in the countryside gives him a new lease of life.

## APOGÉE

*L'apogée de sa carrière est survenu au début des années 80.*[15] – Masculine noun. See also LYCÉE.

## APOSTROPHE

*Cette apostrophe est recommandée en anglais pour marquer le cas possessif.*[16] – Feminine noun.

## APPÂT / APPAS

*Appât* is the bait attached to a hook to catch fish:

*Une mouche fluorescente sert d'appât pour attraper la truite.*[17]

In the figurative sense, it means the lure for something (*l'appât du gain*).

The plural *appas* refers to a woman's charms:

*Les appas de la vamp l'attirent dans ses filets.*[18]

*« C'était, ma foi, un beau brin de fille ; elle avait cinq pieds et quelques pouces et une vraie moisson d'appas. Quelles Vénus que ces Flamandes »*,[19] (—Musset, *Il ne faut jurer de rien*, Acte 3, scène 3).

## APPELER

*Je m'appelle Georgina mais lui s'appelait Georges.*

The *'l'* is doubled before a mute *'–e'*.

*N.B.:* In the future simple and present conditional, the *'l'* is doubled throughout the conjugation: *appellerai, appellerais.* When an *'e'* is in a closed syllable, it is pronounced /e/ instead of /ə/:

*il /ap[pel]le/* → closed syllable;

*il /ap[pe[la/* → open syllable /ə/.[20]

GEORGES POMPIDOU

15. He/she reached the peak of his/her career in the early 80s.
16. In English, this apostrophe should be used to indicate the possessive case.
17. A fluorescent fly is used as bait to catch trout.
18. The femme fatale's charms lure him into her snare.
19. Well, she was an attractive girl; she was just over five feet and had a healthy dose of charm. Flemish women are goddesses!
20. Open syllable (i.e. ending in vowel sound) denoted by '['; closed syllable (i.e. ending in consonant sound) denoted by ']'.

The rule works for the whole paradigm and for verbs like *jeter* as well:

*je jet]te / nous je[tons / je jet]terai / je jet]terais.*

## APRÈS-MIDI

*Après-midi* can be masculine or feminine:

*Un* or *Une après-midi pluvieux /pluvieuse.*

## APRÈS QUE

In theory, the rule is:

*Après que* + indicative; *Avant que* + subjunctive.

In practice, however, even though it is considered incorrect, the subjunctive is commonly found after *après que* by analogy with *avant que.*

Sequence of tenses after *après que* :

(a) *Après que je l'ai vue, elle a disparu :*
Used in spoken language and non-narrative written language (letters etc.).

(b) *Après que je l'avais vue, elle avait disparu :*
A special, rare construction, implying in this case that the speaker had only just glimpsed her when she disappeared.

(c) *Après que je l'eus vue, elle disparut :*
A formal construction restricted to writing and, in particular, narration (short stories, novels, history).

(d) *N.B.:* The pluperfect and the imperfect are used to indicate a habit, as in the following example:
*Après qu'elle avait bien mangé, elle s'endormait.*[21]

## ARBORER / ABHORRER

*Elle était entourée d'enfants arborant un large sourire.*[22]

*Ce qu'elle abhorra le plus, ce fut qu'on lui parla en latin.*[23]

These two verbs are always confused, but while *arborer* means 'to display', *abhorrer* implies 'to loathe'.

21. Every time after she had eaten well, she would fall asleep.

22. She was surrounded by children, sporting a large smile.

23. The thing she despised above all else was being spoken to in Latin.

## ARCANE

*Les arcanes profonds de la psychanalyse m'échappent.*[24]

– Masculine noun.

## ARTABAN

*Il est fier comme Artaban.*[25]

Arrogant, presumptuous character in the novel *Cléopâtre* by Gauthier de Costes, seigneur de la Calprenède.

## ARTICLE (Absence of)

*J'ai ressenti un sentiment de plénitude.*[26]

This does not mean plenitude in itself (such as how one would say 'the truth' or 'the good' in general), but rather the sentiment of something that fulfils his /her aspirations and therefore, no article is needed.

## ARTICLE (Before a Name)

*La Marie est allée au marché.*

In familiar language, one can use the definite article (*le, la*) before a person's first name: *la Marie, la Jeanne, le Pierrot.* This emphasizes the unique character of a specifically designated person, while also having an affective connotation. There are also pseudonyms or last names preceded by the definite article – *la Callas, la Castaphiore* – which gives them a popular connotation.

La Callas

## ASSEOIR

*Asseyez-vous /assoyez-vous.*

This verb has two forms in the present, imperfect, future and conditional, and in the present subjunctive. The expressions *asseyez-vous /assoyez-vous* are both perfectly acceptable, but the latter is more archaic. In the future and the conditional, *je m'assoirai(s)* is more common than *je m'assiérai(s)*. In the past historic, the only possible form is *'ils s'assirent'*.

24. The profound mysteries of psychoanalysis escape me.
25. He is as proud as a peacock.
26. I had a feeling of plenitude.

Note also—*Assieds-toi /assois-toi, où tu veux.*

In Canada, the form *assoyez-vous* is more frequently heard.

## ATTENDANT QUE

*Je dormirai en attendant qu'elle vienne.*

It is tempting to use the 'expletive *ne*' after the construction *en attendant que* : however, literary extracts from Grevisse and Goosse's *Bon Usage* show that the practice is *not* to use it after *en attendant que* : *J'attends de votre sincérité que vous me rassurerez,*[27] (—Nodier, *Contes*, 1993, 1619).

## AUBE / AURORE

*Il avait l'habitude de se lever à l'aube.*[28]

*À l'aurore, la jeune fille quitta le village.*[29]

*Aube* : the first glow of the rising sun, the diffuse light which begins to whiten the horizon, and which comes just before *l'aurore. L'aube* is the moment in time at which this first light appears. *Se lever à l'aube.* [Note: *aube* comes from Latin *alba*, 'white'.]

*Aurore* : the light which precedes sunrise.

## AUCUN(E)

*Il ne se faisait aucun souci.*

*Il n'y avait aucune raison de s'inquiéter.*

*Aucuns* is only used with a plural word that has no singular: *aucuns frais*, or in the set expression *D'aucuns* (*pensent /disent que*...).

## AU DIRE DE

*Au dire de son frère, il valait bien la peine d'essayer.*[30]

*Aux dires de ses détracteurs, il ne valait rien.*[31]

Becomes *aux dires* when followed by a plural (*aux dires des témoins*). According to *Le Trésor de la langue française*, *au dire* and *aux dires* can be used with both a singular and plural.

27. I am waiting for the reassurance of your sincerity.
28. He was used to rising at dawn.
29. The young girl left the village at the break of day.
30. According to his/her brother, it was well worth a shot.
31. According to his critics, he was worthless.

## AU REVOIR

*Elle a quitté la pièce sans dire au revoir.*

The expression *au revoir* should be written in two words.

## AUSPICES

*Cette thèse s'annonce sous les meilleurs auspices.*[32]

– Masculine and only used in the plural.

## AUSSITÔT QUE

(a) *Aussitôt qu'il eut dit ces mots, son frère entra :*

Past anterior in one clause, and past historic in the other.

= The action happened once.

(b) *Aussitôt qu'elle avait dit ces mots, l'acteur entrait sur scène :*

The imperfect indicates repetition or habit.

= 'Every time that she…'

(c) *Aussitôt avait-il terminé qu'il partit :*

The past historic indicates that this is not a repeated event.

*Aussitôt que*, as well as *dès que*, *quand*, *lorsque*, and *après que* are normally followed by the past anterior.

The construction with a pluperfect in combination with a past historic in the main clause is nonstandard.

One should write –

*Il fallait que, aussitôt qu'il était parti, je fasse la vaisselle ;*

– although the following elision is possible:

*Il fallait qu'aussitôt qu'il était parti, je fasse la vaisselle.*

## AUSSITÔT QUE / DÈS QUE

*Aussitôt qu'elle fut partie, j'allai me coucher.*

*Dès qu'il fit jour, je partis courir.*

*Aussitôt que* and *dès que* are almost interchangeable. *Aussitôt que* is slightly more literary and conveys the idea of emergency.

## AU TEMPS POUR MOI

See Temps.

32. This thesis is looking very promising.

## AUTOROUTE

*La population manifestait contre la construction d'une autoroute à cent mètres du village.*[33] Feminine word.

## AU VU DE

*Il fut accepté à l'université au vu de ses bons résultats.*[34]

A set phrase, and therefore invariable.

## AVANT QUE

*Avant que* + subjunctive (using this mode of the hypothetical, we imagine the action which has not yet happened; compare with *après que* which is followed by the indicative).

Sequence of tenses after *avant que* :

(a) Main verb in the present or future –
*Elle ne comprend pas la question avant que je ne la lui explique* (before the explanation).
*Elle ne comprend pas la question avant que je ne la lui aie expliquée* (before completion of the explanation; the action has taken place).

(b) Main verb in the past tense –
*Elle ne comprenait pas la question avant que je ne la lui expliquasse* (before the explanation).
*Elle ne comprenait pas la question avant que je ne la lui eusse expliquée* (before completion of the explanation; the action has taken place).

(c) *La vue de la petite madeleine ne m'avait rien rappelé avant que je n'y eusse goûté*[35] (main verb in the pluperfect; before completion of the act of tasting).

(d) *La vue de la petite madeleine ne me rappelle rien avant que je n'y aie goûté*[36] (main verb in the present tense; before completion of the act of tasting).

In (informal) spoken language, not all these distinctions are made.

33. The people protested against the construction of a highway a hundred meters from the village.
34. He was offered a place at university, in light of his good results.
35. The little madeleine did not remind me of anything until I tasted it.
36. The little madeleine does not remind me of anything until I taste it.

## AVIGNON

*J'ai séjourné à Avignon /en Avignon.*

The latter construction is now obsolete. Formerly there was a Comté of Avignon, under the protection of the Pope, which only became part of France at the time of the Revolution, hence the construction with *en*, as with feminine names of geographical areas and those starting with a vowel. The archaic construction *en Arles* (with reference to the Kingdom of Arles) is still found.

In his *Observations de la langue françoise* (1672), Gilles Ménage lists the forms « *en Anvers, en Avignon, en Orléans, en Angers, en Alençon* », which in his view are justified in order to avoid a juxtaposition of two vowels. A calque on the Italian *in Roma, in Firenze*, he notes that forms such as the following were commonly found in the 17th century: *en Bordeaux, en Paris, en Rouen, en Toulouse.*

## AVOIR / ÊTRE

The general rule is to conjugate *both* of these verbs (i.e. including *être*) in compound tenses with the auxiliary *avoir*, and to use the auxiliary *être* in certain special cases only.

The auxiliary *être* is used with some verbs of movement (such as *aller*, *venir*, cf. *Marie est tombée*) – and change of state (*naître*, *devenir*, *mourir*).[37]

Some verbs (particularly those of movement) which are normally conjugated with *être*, such as *monter* and *descendre*, are conjugated instead with *avoir* when they are used transitively with a direct object, and change their meaning (e.g. *descendre les bagages* means 'carry the luggage downstairs').

*Courir* is always conjugated with *avoir* : *Elle a couru* (i.e. 'she moved, by running'), *elle a couru des risques.*

37. Each letter of the mnemonic 'Dr & Mrs P. Vandertramp' stands for a verb used with *être* (*descendre, rentrer, mourir, revenir, sortir, passer par, venir, aller, naître, devenir, entrer, retourner, tomber, rester, arriver, monter, partir*).

The same holds for *coûter* : *Cela a coûté cher*, *cette bêtise m'a coûté mon emploi.*

Some verbs which are normally conjugated with *avoir* are conjugated instead with *être* when the speaker wants to stress the result: this is the case for *convenir*, for example –
*Nous étions convenu(e)s d'une date pour notre prochain colloque.*[38]

According to the *TLF*[39], the traditional rule is to employ *convenir* –

(a) with the auxiliary verb *être* in the sense of 'to agree', 'to acknowledge';

(b) with the auxiliary verb *avoir* in the sense of 'being appropriate';

but this rule is not always followed, and usage tends to employ *avoir* as the only auxiliary in both cases.

Reflexive and reciprocal verbs always take the auxiliary *être* (*Ils se sont approchés*).

In the passive voice, the auxiliary *être* is always used (*Ces travaux sont exécutés par...*).[40]

As to whether the use of *avoir* instead of *être* is regional, some verbs of motion are occasionally used with *avoir*, either because of literary archaism or popular usage (*il a sorti très tôt ce matin*).

*Demeurer* is an interesting case, and varies depending on the meaning. See DEMEURER.

38. We agreed on a date for the conference.

39. *Le Trésor de la langue française*

40. This pattern of usage can be explained by the linguistic evolution from Latin to French. In Latin, there was no compound past tense. There was a 'perfect' tense: *feci* for *j'ai fait* ('I have done'). The past participle (passive) in Latin *factus* had the sense of 'having been done'.

In Old French the Latin 'perfect' tense fell out of use, and new constructions came about: *j'ai la maison (ayant été) construite* to render the classical Latin *domum aedificavi*, and *la maison est construite* to render the Latin *domus aedificatur*. From *j'ai la maison construite*, speakers then shifted to *j'ai construit la maison*. The agreement of the past participle with the auxiliary *avoir* when there is a preceding direct object comes from this construction. *Habeo domum aedificatam*, in Vulgar Latin, is the equivalent of *Domum aedificavi* in classical Latin.

## B.A.-BA

*Il connaît le b.a.-ba du chinois et du japonais.*[1]

A trap in *Les Dictées de Bernard Pivot*, this noun, which alludes to the first letters of the alphabet and denotes basic or rudimentary knowledge, has an unusual spelling.[2]

Pivot

## BAILLER / BÂILLER

*Vous me la baillez bien bonne /belle.*[3]

Not to be confused with the verb *bâiller* (to yawn), or with the rarer verb *bayer* ('to waste time dreaming'), *bailler* is from the same root as *béer* (as in *rester bouche bée*) and is used predominantly in the fixed expression *la bailler bonne /belle* ('that's a tall tale').

## BALADE / BALLADE

*Rien de mieux qu'une bonne balade en forêt.*[4]

*Il l'a séduite par cette ballade improvisée à la guitare.*[5]

A *balade* is a walk, and not to be confused with *une ballade* which is a poetic or musical work, from the Old Provençal *ballar* (dance).

## BANAL

*Les sujets de dissertation sont très banals cette année.*

*Banals /banales* are used in the plural for reasons of euphony.

1. He knows the basics of Chinese and Japanese.
2. Also spelled in a variety of ways: '*B.A. BA*' [*Le Trésor*], '*le b a ba*' [Hachette], etc.
3. You are trying to pull the wool over my eyes.
4. There is nothing better than a good walk in the forest.
5. He seduced her with this improvised guitar ballad.

## BASILIC / BASILIQUE

*Le basilic* : a plant ('basil'):
*J'ai dégusté une salade assaisonnée de basilic.*[6]
*Le basilic* : Also a mythological reptile ('basilisk'):
*Satan, tel un basilic, séduit et hypnotise Eve par le regard.*[7]
*La basilique*: a religious building ('basilica'): *J'ai visité la basilique du Sacré-Cœur à Paris.*[8]

## BATH

*Quand elle est bath ça va tout seul. Quand elle est moche on s'habitue.* (—Ferré, *Vingt ans*).[9]

This old-fashioned adjective, which comes from slang and means 'pretty' or 'agreeable', is invariable in form.

## BEL ET BIEN

*Elle a eu bel et bien raison de le suivre.*[10]

*Bel et bien* is a set phrase.

*Bel* is used before a word that starts with a vowel.

In idioms, before 'and', the literary usage allows *bel :* e.g. *Tout ce qui est bel et bon*.[11]

## BÉNI / BÉNIT

*Bénit(e)* is only used as an adjective:
*De l'eau bénite /du pain bénit.*
*Béni(e)* is only used as a past participle:
*L'eau a été bénie /le pain a été béni.*

6. I savoured a salad seasoned with basil.
7. Satan, like a basilisk, seduces and hypnotises Eve with a glance.
8. I visited the Basilica of the Sacré-Cœur in Paris.
9. When she is pretty, there is no problem.
   When she is bad, we get used to it.
10. She was absolutely right to follow him.
11. All that is beautiful and good.

## BENJAMIN / CADET

*Elle est la benjamine. Il est le cadet de la famille.*

*Benjamin :* Youngest child of a family or group.

*Cadet :* Child who is not the oldest of his /her family; child immediately after the oldest.

## BERNARD-L'(H)ERMITE

*J'ai trouvé un petit bernard-l'ermite sur la plage.*[12]

This is an expression taken from Languedoc Occitan. The proper name *Bernard* was widely used in the 16th century to describe different animals. We find spelling variations such as *bernard l'ermite /bernard-l'hermite /bernard l'hermite.*

## BIEN / BON

*Ce film est bien /bon.*

Although we tend to use *bon* for food (*ce plat est bon*), the two forms are near equivalents. The former is slightly colloquial.

*Une fille bien* is a girl who is well-brought-up, well educated, behaves properly, and is honest and respectful toward others.

*Une fille bonne* is a girl with a big heart and who acts with goodness and generosity in all that she does. This is the opposite of a mean and selfish girl.

*Bien* (superlative – *le mieux*) is an adverb.

*Bon* (superlative – *le meilleur*) is an adjective.

The word *bien* also exists as a noun (*le bien*, *un bien*, *les biens*, *des biens*). So does *bon* (e.g. as in 'un bon de commande').

Note: *le mieux* behaves like a singular pronoun with the sense of 'the best thing': *Le mieux serait de partir très tôt.*

*Le Petit Robert* considers *mieux* an adjective in:

*Prenez ce siège : vous serez mieux.*

## BIENNAL(E)

*Les préparatifs de cet événement biennal ont demandé des mois de travail.*[13] The adjective *biennal(e)* (with two 'n's) means something that lasts two years, or which happens every two years.

The noun is *biennale : la biennale de Venise.*

12. I found a small hermit crab on the beach.

13. Preparations for this biennial event required months of work.

## BIEN QUE

*Bien qu'il pleuve, nous pourrions aller nous détendre en nous promenant dans la lande.*[14]

Why is *bien que* followed by the subjunctive? [The rule according to which the indicative is used for facts considered to be real is not applied in absolutely every case.]

—In written language, the subjunctive is normally used with *bien que*.

—In spoken language, in Quebec in particular, the indicative is sometimes found.

The notion of concession seems to take precedence over the notion of factuality.

H. Bonnard explains the subjunctive by saying that it « *semble exprimer l'attitude d'esprit qui rejette (fictivement) du réel un phénomène que l'effet dément* »[15] (1971-1978, p.854). Brunot describes this phenomenon as « *servitude grammaticale* » (1936, p.866), which is in line with Judge and Healey's idea of harmonizing subjunctives (1985, p.131). There are cases where the subjunctive is compulsory, as it is conditioned by a set phrase (*il faut que, il n'est pas rare que*, for instance) or a conjunction (*avant que*, *de peur que*, etc.). For them, *bien que* requires a subjunctive because it involves 'an idea of supposition or conjecture' (1985, p.146).

## BILLET / TICKET

*As-tu réservé ton billet de train pour Toulouse?*
*J'ai oublié d'acheter un carnet de tickets de métro.*[16]

The English word *ticket* comes from Old French *estiquet* (French *billet de logement* = English *billet*).

The modern-day French word *ticket* comes from the English word. It has a less general meaning than *billet*, designating a coupon or piece of paper that entitles the holder to a service of some sort. In general usage, and especially in Canada, *billet* can be used in place of *ticket*.

14. Despite the rain, we could go for a relaxing walk in the heath.
15. 'The subjunctive seems to express the attitude of mind that rejects (fictitiously) a phenomenon from reality that the effect denies.'
16. I forgot to buy a book of metro tickets.

In earlier periods, *ticket* was avoided in Canadian French as it was considered an English word. Nowadays, the French influence on Quebec means that *ticket* is commonly used.

## BLESSER / BERCER

Ferré

*Les sanglots longs*
*Des violons*
*De l'automne*
*Blessent mon cœur*
*D'une langueur*
*Monotone.*[17]

Verlaine's famous verse from *Chanson d'automne* (1866) published in *Poèmes saturniens* has been reused and slightly altered in Trenet's song (*Verlaine*, first recorded in 1941), *'blessent mon coeur'* becoming *'bercent mon coeur'*. Brassens' eponymous rendition uses the original *'blessent'*.

Gainsbourg later paraphrased Verlaine's poem several times in his song *Je suis venu te dire que je m'en vais* (1973):

*Je suis venu te dire que je m'en vais* [Verlaine: *'et je m'en vais'*] *//Et tes larmes n'y pourront rien changer. // Comme dit si bien Verlaine au vent mauvais //Je suis venu te dire que je m'en vais //Tu t'souviens des jours anciens et tu pleures* [V.: *'je me souviens des jours anciens et je pleure'*] *//Tu suffoques, tu blêmis à présent qu'a sonné l'heure*[18] [V.: *'tout suffocant et blême quand sonne l'heure'*].

In 1974, Ferré's jazzy version of *Verlaine – Chanson d'automne* uses *'bercent'* in the first stanza and reverts to *'blessent'* in the final stanza. The words obviously vary according to the interpretations each singer made.[19]

17. The long sobs of autumn's violins
wound my heart with a monotonous languor.

18. I came to tell you that I am going away //And your tears will not change anything. //As Verlaine puts it 'in the rough wind' //I came to tell you that I am going away //You remember the old days and you cry //You choke, you turn pale now that the time has come.

19. A version by Trenet uses *'blessent'*.

Broadcast by the BBC in June 1944, Verlaine's verse was used to announce the imminence of the Normandy landings to the French Resistance.

## BLOG

*A ses heures perdues, c'est un blogueur invétéré.*[20]

*Bloggeur* is formed from the English word blogger.

*Blogueur* is formed from the word blog.

Both spellings are acceptable.

## BOIS

*Ils sont allés aux bois cueillir des girolles.*[21]

The song goes: « *Nous n'irons plus aux bois, les lauriers sont coupés…* »[22]

If it is a single wood, we would of course write *au bois*. If it is more than one wood, or woods in general, usage varies.

We say *Ces peuples vivaient dans la forêt*, even if there are several forests.

In Canada, *coureurs des bois* ('fur traders') are those who had to go to the 'Indians', by passing through the forests far to the north of the Great Lakes (for fear of the Iroquois to the south of the Great Lakes). Many French people who do not know the historical meaning of the expression say *les coureurs de bois*.

IROQUOIS

If there are several specific woods, it is better to write *aux bois*. If they are woods in general, both *au bois* and *aux bois* are acceptable.

20. During his off hours, he is an inveterate blogger.
21. They went to the woods to pick chanterelles.
22. We'll go to the woods no more //The laurels have been cut.

## BON

*Les marronniers sentaient si bon.*[23]

*Bon* here is not an attribute of the subject directly. *Sentir bon* is a verbal expression meaning 'to smell good'. Rather, the word *bon* has an adverbial value, qualifying the verb (cf. *bonnement*, *de bonne manière*) : *Cette chemise sent bon.*

See also BIEN [and see also CHÂTAIGNE/MARRON].

## BOUILLON / POTAGE / SOUPE

*Bouillon :* broth or stock, in which solid ingredients have been cooked and strained off after being reduced to a pulp (*'bouillie'*), either served as a simple soup or forming the basis of a sauce. [The more 'finished' *consommé* is a clear liquid that results from clarifying the stock.]

*Potage :* a more or less liquid form of boiled ingredients (vegetables, meat, etc.) in chunks or puréed, which is usually served hot (more refined than a *soupe*).

*Soupe :* a thick and hearty dish, generally served hot, to which solid ingredients (pieces of meat, vegetables, fish, bread, etc.) have been added. It is less liquid than a *potage*. A very rich soup can constitute a meal in a bowl. The word is related to the noun *souper*. Centuries ago among French peasants, *souper* (now called *dîner*) often consisted of a *soupe*.

A *bouillon* is therefore more dilute than a *potage*, which itself is more dilute than a *soupe*.

*Potage* and *soupe* are sometimes confused. In Canada, the word *soupe* is often used with the sense of *potage*. The evening meal is traditionally *le souper*.

ESCOFFIER

## BONHOMME

*Elle est effrayée par les bonshommes de neige.*[24]

*Bonhomme* becomes *bonshommes* in the plural (in spoken French *bonhommes* is frequently used).

23. The chestnut trees smelt so good.
24. She is terrified of snowmen.

## BOUQUIN

*Il est chouette ce bouquin sur les poètes romantiques.*[25]

BAUDELAIRE

The word *bouquin* comes from the Dutch *boek* ('book').English, German, and Dutch are Germanic languages and the words they use for 'book' (*book, Buch, boek*) comes from the same Germanic root **bōk-*. Hence, we can say that the French word *bouquin* and the English word *book* are related, although not directly.

## BRUXELLES

*Je n'arrive pas à lui faire aimer les choux de Bruxelles.*[26]

Usually pronounced /brysɛl/. The word would only have been pronounced with a /ks/ sound in French from the 18th century, contrary to usage in Brussels itself.

## BUT

*Ils ont gagné par trois buts à zéro.*

Is the *'t'* in *but* pronounced?

—There is no rule which says that the *'t'* in *but* has to be pronounced. In Quebec, the *'t'* in *but*, like the *'t'* in *fait*, is typically not pronounced.

The example sentence is commonly pronounced: « *ils ont gagné par trois buTAzéro* ». Logic calls for the pronunciation « *ils ont gagné par trois buZAzéro* », as this is a liaison. The *'s'* is pronounced to avoid the hiatus.

Some linguistic fashions, like the pronunciation of the *'t'* in *but*, are instigated by some speakers and are spread through the media, and end up becoming normal usage.

25. This is a great book about Romantic poets.
26. I cannot manage to persuade him to like Brussels sprouts.

## ÇÀ ET LÀ

*Il a jeté ses affaires çà et là.*

The word *çà* which is now an archaism for *ici* (not to be confused with *ça*) is written with a grave accent.

## CACAHOUÈTE

*Je raffole du beurre de cacahouètes.*[1]

The word derives from the Mexican *cacahuatl* (meaning *cacao* in the Náhuatl language of the Aztecs). *Cacahouète*, *cacahuète*, and *cacahouette* are also acceptable.

The nursery rhyme *Pirouette cacahouète* plays on the assonance between the two words and is often translated as *Pirouette peanut butter.*

## CANAL

*J'aime naviguer le long des canaux d'Amsterdam.*[2]

Becomes *canaux* in the plural.

SHAKESPEARE

## CAPITAL LETTERS

*Les écrivains anglais ont énormément influencé la poésie française : des références à Shakespeare, Milton, Keats ou Shelley y sont omniprésentes.*[3]

One must go back to the Roman era to find the origins of the capital letter, with capital letters carved on stones, and lowercase letters later written on softer material such as papyrus. The Romans had 21 letters that were first written in capitals: A, B, C, D, E, F, G, H, I, K, L, M, N, O, P, Q, R, S, T, V, X, with 'Y' and 'Z' added later for writing words of Greek origin, and the letters 'J' and 'U' introduced in the Middle Ages (to distinguish the vowel and consonant usages of

1. I love peanut butter.
2. I like to sail along the canals in Amsterdam.
3. English writers have greatly influenced French poetry: it contains perpetual allusions to Shakespeare, Milton, Keats, or Shelley.

'I' and 'V').[4] *'W'* appears in French in adopted Germanic words.

Surnames in French are often written all in capitals (to make clear which name is the family name), but otherwise capitals are used less frequently than in English: initial capitals are not used for days of the week, months, languages, nationality, addresses (apart from proper names in them), religions, etc. Headings and titles generally appear with just the first word (and any proper names) capitalized – unless the first word is the definite article *'Le' 'La' 'L'' 'Les'*, in which case it and its noun and any intervening adjective are all capitalized, or unless the title contains nouns of equal weight (in which case both nouns are capitalized, *'La Guerre et la Paix'*). In French, there is no capital letter after a colon which can occur in English (especially in American English).

There has been debate (started by *Vogue* magazine two decades ago) as to whether capital letters should be accented. According to the *Académie*, accents should always be used on capitals. It is debated as to whether to change French keyboards to make the use of accented capitals easier (*'réforme de l'azerty'*).

ÉRIK ORSENNA
ACADÉMICIEN

## CAR / PARCE QUE

*Nous ne sortirons pas car il pleut/parce qu'il pleut.*

Although stylistically *car* is often preferred to *parce que* in literary contexts, the former is grammatically a coordinating conjunction while the latter is subordinating conjunction. *Car* puts two clauses on the same level, while *parce que* establishes a hierarchy, emphasizing the cause as in the example above.

*Car*, unlike *parce que*, cannot be used at the start of a sentence: *Parce qu'il n'a jamais goûté aux huîtres, il est persuadé que c'est mauvais.*

## CARDINAL

*Le pape va nommer ses cardinaux.*

*Cardinaux* is the plural of *cardinal.*

*Les cardinals* are a type of passerine bird.

4. For more detail see: http://www.tusculan.com/latin/alphalatinphp

## CAS

*Je me prépare au cas où il viendrait.*

Why do we use the conditional rather than the imperfect after *au cas où*?

—The expression *au cas où* is synonymous with *si* which does take the imperfect.

The use of *si* + imperfect followed by the present conditional and also *si* + pluperfect followed by the past conditional are special constructions. They are used to render the following cases in Latin:

(a) potentiality, which in Latin requires the present subjunctive in both clauses (cf. *si j'étais avec vous, je serais heureux* – in Latin: *si sim vobiscum, sim felix*). These uses of the subjunctive for hypothetical events in French can be found as early as the Middle Ages.

(b) the hypothetical present, which in Latin requires the imperfect subjunctive in both clauses (cf. *si tu es avec nous, tu es heureux* – in Latin: *si essem vobiscum, essem felix*).

(c) the hypothetical past, which in Latin requires the pluperfect subjunctive in both clauses (cf. *si j'avais été avec vous, j'aurais été heureux* – in Latin: *si fuissem vobiscum, fuissem felix*).

## CECI / CELA / C'EST

*Ceci /cela est vrai /c'est vrai.*

In general, to say whether something is considered to be true or not, we say simply *c'est vrai* or *c'est faux*.

For something which has just been said, shown or read, we say *cela est vrai*. The same is true for something which can be seen at a distance (e.g. on a poster).

For something which one is about to say, we use *ceci (ce que je vais dire) est vrai*.

To contrast two things, we say *cela est vrai, mais ceci est faux*, or vice versa. *Ceci* designates the last-mentioned thing.

## CEDILLA

The cedilla is placed on the *'c'* immediately before the vowels *'a'*, *'o'*, *'u'* to give it an /s/ sound: *une leçon*, *un hameçon*, *un maçon*.

According to Dubois (2002), the cedilla first appeared *« dès le VIII$^{e}$ siècle dans les manuscrits wisigothiques, mais elle fut peu utilisée par les scribes, qui préféraient employer une lettre supplémentaire pour noter le son sifflant de c (ils écrivaient receut, aperceut) »*.[5]

## CENSÉ / SENSÉ

*Il est censé partir à 2 heures.*
*Je trouve les paroles du ministre sensées.*

*Censé* (from Latin *censeo*: to think, consider that): 'be supposed /presumed that…'

*Sensé* from *sens*: 'which makes sense', 'wise'.

## CENT / VINGT / MILLE

We write *quatre cents*, *quatre-vingts* with an '*s*', but *quatre cent un* and *quatre-vingt-dix* without.

For all figures below 100, a hyphen is used, except when the digits are connected by *et* :

*vingt et un* but *vingt-deux.*

Is the rule about the invariability of *cent* and *vingt* purely arbitrary?

—Although *viginti* and *centum* are invariable in Latin, *Vingt* and *cent 'variaient ordinairement autrefois dans les multiples, même s'ils étaient suivis d'un adjectif numéral' : « Ce premier de mars mille cinq cens quatre vingts »* (—Montaigne, *Essais. Au lecteur*); *« Mil cinq cents quatre-vingts neuf »* (—Guez de Balzac, *Dissert. critiques*, VI, 3).

Montaigne

In 1762, the Academy still wrote *neuf cents mille.* The current practice, established in the 18$^{th}$ century, was arbitrarily imposed by grammarians (see Grevisse and Goosse: 1993, 894).

*Million* and *milliard* agree for number (*millions*, *milliards*), whereas the number *mille* is invariable (*gagner des mille et des cents*). See also Mille, Vingt.

5. Quoted in http://www.etudes-litteraires.com/langue-francaise/origine-cedille.php

## CE QUI / CE QU'IL

*Fais ce qui te plaît /ce qu'il te plaît.*

Both are correct, although there is a small distinction in meaning. *Fais ce qui te plaît* (i.e. 'do the thing that pleases you') or *fais ce qu'il te plaît* (*…de faire*, implicit). Similarly, we write *ce qui advint…* or *ce qu'il advint fut plutôt drôle.*

Impersonal structures occur frequently with verbs such as *se passer*, *arriver*, *advenir*, (*je lui ai demandé ce qu'il se passe*), although *je lui ai demandé ce qui se passe* is more commonly used.

## CERF / CLEF

*Le parc regorge de cerfs de toute beauté.*[6]

*As-tu perdu les clefs ?*

The *'f'* is silent. The (unvoiced) *'f'* comes from the (voiced) *'v'* consonants in the Latin *cervus*, *clavis*. Think of *cervidé.*

The pronunciation of *cerf* as /sɛʁ/ corresponds to the most common usage (the final *'f'* is not pronounced in either the singular or the plural): however, some dictionaries allow /sɛʁf/ and the resulting liaison.

The homophone *serf* is unrelated: this denotes a peasant who worked on the land of a feudal lord. The word *servage* comes from the Latin *servus* (*C'est au Moyen Age que les serfs devaient travailler dur dans les champs pour gagner leur pain*).

## CERNE

*Elle avait des cernes noirs sous les yeux.*

*Cerne* ('ring') is masculine.

## C'EST / CE SONT

*C'est /Ce sont les étudiants français qui ont le mieux réussi.*

The former construction is more typical of the spoken register. The latter, which shows plural agreement, is more elaborate and is recommended in writing.

Similarly, we would write: *c'étaient de studieuses journées qui l'attendaient à l'université.*

6. The park has a plethora of magnificent deer.

## C'ÉTAIT

Purists recommend not writing *c'était que…*, even though it is used in speech.

Searching on the internet for the words to the Canadian song *Le petit bonheur* by Félix Leclerc, which starts « *C'est un petit bonheur que j'avais rencontré* », we find several versions of the song starting « *C'était un petit bonheur que j'avais rencontré* », which is not what the songwriter actually sings.

LECLERC

## C'EÛT

*C'eût été préférable qu'il se taise.*[7]

Elided form of *cela eût*, used before a vowel.

This is the second form of the past conditional, a literary alternative to the first form of the past conditional (*ç'aurait été*).

## CHACAL

*Il a aperçu une meute de chacals.*[8]

The grammatical rule states that words ending with '*-al*' become '*-aux*' in the plural. *Chacal* is an exception and becomes *chacals* in the plural, like *bal* and *carnaval.*

## CHACUN

*Elles sont venues chacune avec un copain.*
*Il y a dans cette analyse trois parties introduites chacune par une citation.*

*Chacun* remains in the singular regardless of the subject of the verb.

## CHAIR / CHAIRE / CHÈRE

*Ce que je préfère c'est la chair d'un fruit bien juteux pour me désaltérer.*[9]

*Chair* denotes flesh, the edible part of an animal or a fruit.

*Une chaire* is a professorial post in a university, or the seat

7. It would have been better if he had kept quiet.
8. He saw a pack of jackals.
9. Nothing quenches my thirst like the flesh of a juicy piece of fruit.

of an ecclesiastic: *Il vient d'obtenir une chaire de professeur à l'université de Rennes.*[10] [We say *chaise* in French, because of a phenomenon of rhotacism[11] that changed the word after the English borrowed the word *chair* from French.]

We write *faire bonne chère* (for bodily and sensory pleasure): *Voilà une belle merveille que de faire bonne chère avec bien de l'argent* (—Molière, *L'Avare*). [Here the noun *chère* ('face') – *chiere* in Old French – came from late Latin 'cara' and Greek κάρᾱ ('head').[12]] Originally the phrase meant *faire bon visage*, but the meaning slipped because of the homonymy.

## CHAMALLOWS

*Mes enfants adorent manger des Chamallows.*

The word *Chamallows* is a trade name whose sound recalls the English word *marshmallow.*

## CHAPITRE

*On trouve une référence à Shakespeare dans le troisième chapitre de cet ouvrage.*

Words ending in *-itre* like *pupitre* do not normally take a circumflex: the exceptions are *un bélître*, *une épître* and *une huître*.

## CHÂTAIGNE / MARRON

*Le 'marron' est une variété de châtaigne, appelée ainsi car il ressemble au marron d'Inde, fruit du marronnier, qui lui ne se mange pas.*

The tree *Castanea Sativa* (called *Châtaignier* in French) is the tree that produces edible chestnuts, and the tree *Aesculus Hippocastanum* (called *Marronier d'Inde* in French, and Horse Chestnut in English) produces inedible chestnuts (sometimes called 'conkers' in English). Strictly speaking, for botanists, *marron* is the inedible fruit of the *Marronnier d'Inde*. [The bur (*la bogue* in French) of the *châtaigne* contains the fruits separated from each other in brownish casings. The bur of the *marron* contains an undivided nut.]

10. He has just obtained a professorship at the University of Rennes.

11. [The change of a consonant into an 'r' sound.]

12. *Dictionnaire Gaffiot (latin-français)*; *Glossarium Du Cange*, etc.

However, the words *marrons* (or *marrons comestibles*) and *châtaignes* are used interchangeably in French gastronomy recipes (Faugier's tins of *marrons* produced in Privas, and the *marrons glacés* for example). In English cookbooks, 'marron' refers to the edible fruit.

As a colour adjective, *châtaigne* remains invariable: *des yeux châtaigne.*

## CHÂTAIN

*Elle avait les cheveux châtains.*

*Châtain* comes from *châtaigne*. However, it agrees in gender and number: *des chevelures châtaines.* It remains invariable when it is a compound adjective: *des tresses châtain clair, châtain-roux* (with hyphen because *roux* is a colour adjective).

## CHÈVRE

*J'adore l'histoire de la chèvre de Monsieur Seguin d'Alphonse Daudet.*

Takes a grave accent rather than a circumflex. The accent is here to make the *e* sound /e/ instead of /ə/.

DAUDET

## CHEZ

To designate a shop or other establishment, we use the preposition '*à*' : we go *à la boulangerie.* The *à* (*au*) in *Je te retrouve au cinéma* implies 'at the cinema', while *Je te retrouve dans le cinéma* implies inside the cinema building.

To refer to the manager or owner of an establishment, we use the preposition *chez* : e.g. *on va chez le docteur.* However, when I say *je vais chez le coiffeur*, I do not necessarily want to say that I am going to see the owner of the hair salon, but simply that I am going to get a haircut. Indeed, although most people who practice this profession are women, the feminine is not used for that: (… *j'irai chez la coiffeuse* is incorrect), which indicates that it is not the person herself that one seeks to designate… It is always *à* + location (*Avant de rentrer je passerai à la boucherie*) and *chez* + the person (*Avant de rentrer je passerai chez le boucher*) : the grammatical construction is different, but from a pragmatic point of view, both sentences refer to the same action of buying meat.

The preposition *chez* comes from the Latin *casa* ('the house of...').

## CHIC

*Ils portent des toilettes très chic.*

This adjective is normally invariable.

## CHOCOLATINE

*J'ai acheté trois chocolatines.*

The debate between *pain au chocolat* and *chocolatine* has been in the media in France. According to statistics, the use of *chocolatine* is mostly regional and used in the south-west.

In Quebec, the latter is used.

## CHOIR

*Il laissa choir son stylo à un moment particulièrement important de la discussion.*[13]

The future tense form of the rare verb *choir* ('to fall') is *cherra*.

*Tire la chevillette et la bobinette cherra*[14] is the Big Bad Wolf's famous expression to Little Red Riding Hood in Perrault's fairy story. The past participle is *chu* : cf. *ange déchu.*

## CHYPRE (AND OTHER ISLANDS)

*Elle se rendra à Chypre pour les grandes vacances.*

In French, one normally uses the preposition *à* before the names of islands: *aller à Chypre, à Cuba, à Hawaï, à la Martinique, à la Guadeloupe*, but it should be *en Corse, en Sardaigne, en Crète, en Sicile* (it is because these islands being closer and more familiar to French speakers are considered in the stretch of their land, as a region, rather than a little point on the globe).

The usage of the preposition in the case of *Martinique* is fluctuating. *À la* is prescribed, but in common usage *en* is used.

13. He dropped his pen at a particularly important moment in the discussion.

14. Pull the bobbin and the latch will go up.

## CIEL

*Son regard se tourna vers les cieux.*
*Les ciels de Titien sont d'un bleu de toute beauté.*[15]

The plural *les cieux* has a religious sense. *Les ciels* is used in the context of painting. Other double plurals include: *aïeux/aïeuls* (ancestors /grandparents), *yeux/œils-*, *travaux/travails*.

Le Titien

## CIME

*C'est à la cime de l'arbre qu'il est monté.*

There is no circumflex on *cime* ('top'), as the mnemonic and jocular sentence *le chapeau de cime est tombé dans l'abîme* reminds us. See Abîme.

## CIRCUMFLEX

The circumflex, consisting of an acute accent and a grave accent, would have appeared for the first time in French in the 16th century and came from the ancient Greek. It would only be in the 18th century that its usage was normalized.

(a) The circumflex accent is retained in some parts of verb conjugation:
in 1st and 2nd person plural of the past historic:
*fûmes*, *fûtes*, *eûmes*, *eûtes*, etc.
in 3rd person singular of the imperfect subjunctive:
*fût*, *eût*, *parlât*, etc.

(b) The circumflex stands for an original 's' in Latin before another consonant (*fusmes, fustes*). In many words it marks the suppression in the 17th or 18th century of an 's' which was by that time no longer pronounced*: *forêt*, *pâte*, *hôtel* :

| | |
|---|---|
| *forêt* | from Anglo-Latin *foresta* |
| *île* | from *insula* |
| *hôtel* | from medieval Latin *hospitale* |
| *hôpital* | from *hospitalis* |
| *hôte* | from *hospes/hospita* |

[*English, which borrowed a lot of French words because French was the language of the court after the Battle of Hastings, has kept this 's' because it was still pronounced in Old French when it came into the language.]

15. Titian's skies are a magnificent blue.

(c) With *paraître*, the circumflex only appears before the '*t*' because the '*s*' would not disappear in front of another '*s*' : *je parais, nous paraissions* as opposed to *je paraîtrai, tu paraîtrais...*
(d) The circumflex serves to distinguish the homophone pairs: *dû* (participle) and *du* (article); *croît /crût /crû* (present, past historic and past participle of *croître*) and *croit /crut /cru* (present, past historic and past participle of *croire*).

During the Middle Ages, some sounds disappeared (for example, '*maistre*' became '*maître*'), and this disappearance brought about the lengthening of the preceding vowel. In the Renaissance, typographers and lexicographers borrowed the circumflex from Greek to mark this accentuation. Usage then fluctuated. In the third edition of the *Dictionnaire de l'Académie* (1740) the usage was generalised.

Why is there no circumflex to distinguish *il a plu* (from *pleuvoir*) from *cela lui a plu* (from *plaire*)?

—It is not essential to avoid homography at all costs. Here, context is usually enough to allow language users to distinguish easily between *a plu* (from *pleuvoir*) et *a plu* (from *plaire*).

On the other hand, since the article *du* is so frequently used, the past participle of the verb *devoir*, its homograph *dû*, takes a circumflex.

Ambiguity is possible with *cru* and *crû*. However, there is no accent on the *u* of *accru*.

## CITRON

As a colour adjective, *citron* is invariable: *des draps citron.*

## CLÉ / CLEF

*J'ai retrouvé mes clés /clefs de voiture.*

The words *clé /clef* come from Latin *clavis* ('key'). There was probably a period when the pronunciations /cle/ and /clɛ/ were both heard (with the voiced /v/ becoming the unvoiced /f/). Think of *clavier*.

## CLÉMENTINE / MANDARINE

*Les clémentines et les mandarines sont des fruits riches en vitamines C.*

*La clémentine* is a cross between a tangerine and a sweet orange.

*La mandarine* is the fruit of the mandarin tree.

*La mandarine satsuma* is a variety of mandarin.

*La tangerine* is a cross between a mandarin and a bitter orange.

## COI

*Nous sommes restées coites.*[16]

The feminine form is *coite* ; the masculine plural *cois* and the feminine plural *coites.*

## COIFFEUR

*Je vais chez le coiffeur une fois par mois.*

With a person, we use the preposition *chez*. See CHEZ.

ANTOINE DE PARIS

## COMMA

The comma precedes *qui* if the relative clause is explanatory and not determinative. For example:

*Cet individu, qui me ressemble, est mon cousin* (explanatory).[17]

*L'individu qui a commis ce crime a été arrêté* (determinative).[18]

*Les Français, qui boivent du vin rouge, ont moins de maladies cardiaques que les Finlandais.* ('The French in general have less heart disease than the Finnish, because they drink more red wine.') – the appositive relative clause gives an explanation for the information given in the main clause.

*Les Français qui boivent du vin rouge ont moins de maladies cardiaques.* ('Only the French people who drink red wine [i.e. not all the French] have less heart disease.') – the determinative relative clause delimits a subcategory of French people to which the sentence applies.

It is difficult to establish the origin of the comma. The

16. We kept still /silent.
17. This individual, who resembles me, is my cousin.
18. The individual who has committed this crime has been arrested.

most plausible hypothesis is that it reached us from Italian printers who themselves would have borrowed it from Arabic writing (Mourad: 2003).

## COMMENCER DE / À

A number of verbs (*commencer*, *contraindre*, *obliger*, *s'efforcer*, *s'ennuyer*, *continuer*, *faire attention*, etc.) are connected to the following infinitive with either *à* or *de* : the choice of one or other depends on the sound of the sentence. As Grevisse and Goosse (1993, 1282) suggest, in these cases it is the ear which decides.

## COMPOUND NOUN (PLURAL)

Compound nouns are used with a hyphen and their plurals vary according to their patterns:

(a) Adverb + Noun:

*Une arrière-boutique ; un demi-tarif ; un non-lieu.*
– The adverb remains invariable:
*des arrière-boutiques ; des demi-tarifs ; des non-lieux.*

(b) Noun + Adjective /Adjective + Noun:

*Un coffre-fort ; une grand-mère ; une plate-bande.*
– Both elements take the plural:
*des coffres-forts ; des grands-mères ; des plates-bandes.*

(c) Noun + Noun:

*un bateau-mouche ; un chou-fleur ; un mot-clé.*
– Both nouns take the mark of the plural:
*des bateaux-mouches ; des choux-fleurs ; des mots-clés.*
It should however be *des timbres-poste* (meaning *de la poste*).

(d) Noun + Prepositional Phrase:

*Un arc-en-ciel; un chef d'œuvre; une pomme de terre.*
– The first noun only becomes plural:
*des arcs-en-ciel ; des chefs d'œuvre ; des pommes de terre.*
*Des pot-au-feu* and *des tête-à-tête* are exceptions that remain invariable.

(e) Verb + Noun:

*un gratte-ciel ; un ouvre-boîte ; un porte-monnaie.*
– The verb remains invariable in the plural:
*des gratte-ciel ; des ouvre-boîte ; des porte-monnaie.*

(f) Verbal Phrasal Compounds:

*Un manque-à-gagner ; un on-dit ; un va-et-vient.*

– It remains invariable:

*des manque à gagner ; des on-dit ; des va-et-vient.*

## CONCERNER

*En ce qui concerne mes parents…*

The pronouns *ceci*, *cela*, *rien*, *ce qui*, etc. are always singular. In the example above, the subject of *concerne* is *ce qui*.

## CONDITIONAL PAST (SECOND FORM)

See Pluperfect Subjunctive

## CONDITIONAL / SUBJUNCTIVE

*Quels que soient les livres que tu choisirais /choisisses, il faudra que tu demandes la permission à la bibliothécaire.*[19]

(a) *Que tu choisirais* implies an explicit or implicit condition, i.e. 'if you accompanied me to the library, you would have to choose…'

(b) *Que tu choisisses* implies 'when you choose books, you will have to ask permission' (no matter what the situation is).

## CONFIANCE (FAIRE)

*J'ai confiance dans les médias.*

*Avoir confiance* : to really trust the person concerned.

*Faire confiance* : to decide to trust this person for a specific occasion.

In the construction 'to put one's trust in …', we use the verb *faire* : *'On fait confiance à …'*

'To trust /have confidence in …' takes *avoir* : *'On a confiance en /dans …'*

Before an article, we use *dans* (as in the example above).

Before a personal pronoun referring to a person, it is common to use *en* (*en lui, en elle*).

19. You have to ask the librarian for permission, whichever books you choose.

## CONFIER

*Elle s'est vu confier de nouvelles responsabilités.*[20]

*Se voir confier* that is to say 'to be aware that one is given something'. The pronoun *'se'* is the indirect object.

## CONSEQUENCE

*Elle a eu si peur qu'elle s'est tue* (expression of fear).

When the 'consequence' in the adjoining clause is an actual fact (i.e. something which has already taken place), the verb is in the indicative.

## CONSISTER

*Consister* ***dans***, meaning 'lie in', 'be based in', is followed by a noun: *La bonté consiste dans l'altruisme.* This construction is old-fashioned and literary.

*Consister* ***en***, meaning 'be composed of', is followed by a noun: *Cette cuisine consiste en six chaises et une minuscule table [= est composée de].*

*Consister* ***à***, meaning 'to consist in', is followed by an infinitive.

## CONSONANT (PRONUNCIATION).

See also Août and Ours

*Quelle joie de se plonger dans les anecdotes truculentes de l'almanach Vermot.*[21]

Henriette Walter

As Henriette Walter has shown (1988, 96-98), there is a lot of fluctuation as regards the pronunciation of the final consonant in French with such words as: *almanach, ananas, août, but, cerf, chenil, circonspect, exact, fait (un), gril, nombril, persil, sourcil, suspect.* It seems that the less frequent the word (in the case of *chenil* or *cerf* for instance), the more frequently one tends to pronounce the final consonant almost by hypercorrection. With very frequent words such as *persil* or *sourcil,* one would favour the pronunciation with a mute final consonant.

20. She was given new responsibilities.

21. What a joy to immerse yourself in the colourful anecdotes of Vermot's almanac.

In Quebec, one continues to say *nombril, sourcil, persil, baril* without pronouncing the final '*l*'.

## COORDINATING CONJUNCTION

*Mais où est donc Ornicar ?* is the mnemonic expression drummed into French primary school children to help them remember the French coordinating conjunctions: *mais*, *ou*, *et*, *donc*, *or*, *ni*, *car*. See also ET.

## CORIANDRE

*Cette coriandre est très parfumée.* – Always feminine.

## CORNOUAILLE / CORNOUAILLES

*La Cornouailles possède une végétation méditerranéenne où poussent même des palmiers.*[22]

Etymologically, *Cornouailles* means inhabitants (*ouailles)* of the region of Corn, in reference to the long *horn* of land.

*Cornouailles*, French for Cornwall, should not be confused with its homophone *Cornouaille* without the 's' which is a region in Brittany. *Le cornique* is the French for *Cornish*, the now extinct Celtic language that was spoken in Cornwall.

## CORRECT

*On lui demande d'être politiquement correct.*

The adjectives *correct*, *exact*… do not take an '*e*' in the masculine.

## COUDRE

*Elle coud une robe par jour.*

The past historic of *coudre* is *cousis, cousis, cousit* etc.

## COUP

*On a tout à coup entendu un drôle de bruit.*
*Il est parti tout d'un coup.*

*Tout à coup* means all of a sudden, suddenly.

*Tout d'un coup* means just one time, all at once.

22. Cornwall has Mediterranean vegetation where even palm trees grow.

## COURIR

*La course qu'il a courue ; les 10 kilomètres qu'il a couru.*

Why is the past participle of *courir 'couru'* and not *'couri'* ?

This is about an exception. All exceptions in French can be explained within the framework of the study of the evolution of the language (from Vulgar Latin to modern French). A diachronic analysis of French, such as is done in historic morphology, scientifically accounts for the following of the evolution of the past participle in ancient and middle French.

See also Vivre.

## COÛTER

*La somme que cela a coûtée ; les 15 euros que ce livre a coûté.*

See also Vivre.

## CROCHE-PIED

*Pendant le match de foot, il a dû éviter nombre de croche-pieds de ses adversaires.*[23]

*Croche-pied*[24] takes an *s* in the plural: *des croche-pieds.*

Maître Capello

23. During the football match, he had to avoid being tripped several times by his opponents.

24. A special episode of « Qui veut gagner des millions ? » ('Who Wants to be a Millionaire') in November 2004 caused some amazement, when the famous linguist and popular television star Maître Capello, reputed for being unbeatable in spelling and French grammar, was questioned by humorist Laurent Baffie about the plural of *'croche-pied'*. Maître Capello stated that this word was invariable, but his answer was judged to be incorrect. *Le Petit Larousse* stated that it was variable. However, the Master's advice was perfectly logical and justified, because one trips, generally, a foot; this is one of the most arbitrary conventions: we write *des casse-pieds*, *des chausse-pieds*, but *des crocs en jambe*.

## CROIRE

*Elle croit tout ce qu'on lui dit* (and not « *…en tout ce qu'on lui dit* » which is incorrect).

*Croire une chose* ('to believe something') is to believe that it is true. In the example above, she believes everything that she is told, she believes that people always tell her the truth.

*Croire dans /en une chose* ('to believe *in* something') is to believe that it is possible or that it can succeed or obtain results.

*Tu dois croire en tes possibilités, tes capacités, ton talent.*

*Croire en quelqu'un* ('believe in someone') is to trust that person.

## CROIRE QUE + SUBJUNCTIVE / INDICATIVE

In formal language the indicative is also possible after the negative of *penser* and *croire*. This conveys that the speaker is really sure (s/he has no doubt) about the action of the subordinate clause (*Il ne pense pas que c'est faisable*). However, the subjunctive would be used here in standard French (*Il ne pense pas que ce soit faisable*).

*Il ne pense pas qu'il est faisable de la réparer* : he thinks it is not possible (affirmation: it is not possible).

*Il ne pense pas qu'il soit faisable de la réparer* : he has been led to believe that it cannot be done.

Compare –

*Il ne faudrait pas croire que le romantisme peut se comprendre en dehors du contexte.*

with –

*Il ne faudrait pas croire que le romantisme puisse se comprendre en dehors du contexte.*

There is a subtle difference between the use of the indicative and the subjunctive here. The use of the indicative (*que le romantisme peut se comprendre en dehors du contexte…*) implies that the speaker believes that Romanticism can be understood (that is, it is a fact). The use of subjunctive (*que le romantisme puisse se comprendre en dehors du contexte…*) implies that the speaker believes that Romanticism *could be* explained (e.g. possibly, or under certain conditions).

## CRU / CRÛ

*Cru* is the past participle of the verb *croire* ; *crû* is the past participle of *croître.*

*Il a cru bon de répondre.*

*La plante a crû très vite.*

In the past historic:

*Il crut bon de répondre.*

*La plante crût très vite.*

## CUILLER / CUILLÈRE

*Une cuiller à soupe d'huile de ricin par jour et tu te sentiras beaucoup mieux.*[25]

The spellings *cuiller* and *cuillère* are both perfectly acceptable, but the latter (*cuillère*) is more common.

## CUISSE

*J'adore les cuisses de grenouille.*

*Le Petit Robert* writes *manger des cuisses de grenouilles* and the *Collins Robert* gives *cuisses de grenouilles* as the translation of 'frogs' legs' (i.e. with *grenouilles* pluralised). *Le Petit Larousse* and other dictionaries give *des cuisses de grenouille* (in the singular).

A speaker who uses « *cuisses de grenouille* » (in the singular) considers frog as meat (as in « *cuisses de poulet* »), whereas « *cuisses de grenouilles* » with an '*-s*' implies that the frogs are countable and considered as single entities: *on a attrapé des grenouilles et on va manger des cuisses de grenouilles.*

## CUISSEAU / CUISSOT

*Le cuisinier a préparé un cuissot de chevreuil pour les convives.*[26]

A classic in Prosper Mérimée's dictation: we talk about *cuisseau* of a calf and *cuissot* of a stag, roe deer, or wild boar.

MÉRIMÉE

25. If you have a tablespoon of castor oil a day, you will feel much better.

26. The chef prepared a haunch of venison for the guests.

## DATE BUTOIR

*Ils devront rendre leur dossier avant la date butoir.*

The plural ('deadlines') is *dates butoirs.*

## DATIF ÉTHIQUE (ETHICAL DATIVE[1])

*Elle te lui a donné une de ces leçons.*[2]

*La bouteille de vin, je me la suis bue en entier.*[3]

This is an emphatic use of a personal pronoun (first or second person), in this case, *'te'* or *'me'*. It does not add anything to what is said in the phrase, but it emphasizes the personal position and the affectivity of the speaker in relation to what is announced in the sentence. This usage belongs to familiar language.

## D'AUTRES / DES AUTRES

*D'autres enfants*: 'some other children', 'of some other children' (indefinite). –

*D'autres enfants font la même chose qu'eux :* i.e. other children who did the same thing (indefinite).

*D'autres enfants seraient intimidés, mais pas lui.*

*Des autres enfants :* 'of the other children'. –

*Les actions des autres enfants ne sont pas pires que celles des tiens*[4] (i.e. children who are not yours).

It is not possible to use *des* as a form which is grammatically isolated, as in *des autres enfants seraient intimidés*, because *des*

1. Ethical datives have become a feature of dialectal American English, most particularly in the South and Appalachia, with similar constructions as in French, such as 'they killed him his bird' – '[ethical datives] typically invite benefactive and malefactive (adversative) understandings respectively'. See Mark Liberman and Geoffrey Pullum's language log: http://languagelog.ldc.upenn.edu/nll/?p=1863.
2. I taught him/her a real lesson, you know.
3. I drank that whole bottle of wine to myself.
4. The other children are not behaving any worse than your own.

is a contracted form of *de* + *les*. But compare: *Je ne me souviens pas de Marie, mais je me souviens des autres enfants.*

In more detail –

*Des* (= *Un* /*Une* in the plural form) is Indefinite; for example, *Je vois des enfants dans la foule*, 'I see in the crowd a certain number of individuals that correspond to the definition of the noun *enfant,* but I cannot identify them.' In such cases, if I decide to place an adjective before the noun (*autre*, or any other adjective), *Des* becomes *De* /*D' : d'autres enfants.*

*Des*, a contraction of *De Les* (= *Du* /*De La* made into the plural form), is Definite. For example, *La voix des enfants est très belle :* either I am speaking about a specific group of children, identified in the situation of the utterance; or I am speaking about all children in general.

In such cases, if I decide to place an adjective before the noun, *Des* remains *Des : des autres enfants; La bonne conduite des sages enfants est toujours récompensée.*

Thus –

*Je ne me souviens pas de Marie, mais je me souviens d'autres enfants qui étaient là* ('I do not remember Marie, but I remember the other children who were there'), and

*Je ne me souviens pas de Marie, mais je me souviens des autres enfants qui étaient là* ('I do not remember Marie, but I remember other children who were there'),

– are both grammatically correct, but they do not mean the same thing:

(i) In the first sentence, I remember children without being able to precisely identify them. The equivalent in the singular would be *Je ne me souviens pas de Marie, mais je me souviens d'un(e) autre enfant qui était là* ('I do not remember Marie, but I remember another child who was there').

(ii) In the second sentence, I remember children whose identity I know. The equivalent in the singular would be: *Je ne me souviens pas de Marie, mais je me souviens de l'autre enfant / l'autre petite fille qui était là* ('I do not remember Marie, but I remember the other child /the other little girl who was there').

## DE (ABSENCE OF ARTICLE)

*Elle portait un volant de dentelle.*[5]

de + noun (without an article) denotes the material from which the garment is made (cf. *de soie*, *de laine*, etc. without an article).

## DE / DU

*Je veux du lait. Je ne veux plus de lait.* We use *de* here rather than *du*, because of the negation. *Je ne veux plus de café* means *no more.*

## DÉBARRASSER

*Cette idée, ne s'est-il pas souvenu de s'en être débarrassé ?*[6]

In this sentence, the verb is essentially pronominal. The past participle agrees with the subject.

## DÉCENNIE / DÉCADE

*La planète a connu sa décennie la plus chaude depuis 1880.*[7]
*Après l'agitation de la décade passée, le pays a connu une certaine accalmie.*[8]

*Décennie* is the term that needs to be employed to designate a period of ten years. *Décade* designates the ten day week of the Republican calendar created during the French Revolution.

## DÉCIDER

*Décider + de :* to make a decision to –
*Il a décidé de faire la vaisselle.*
*Décider qqn + à :* to persuade someone to make a decision –
*Elle a décidé son frère à partir.*
Passive form: *Décider + à :*
*Il est décidé à faire des études.*
Pronominal form: *Se décider + à :*
*Elles se sont décidées à vivre seules.*

5. She was wearing a lace flounce.
6. Didn't he remember to forget this idea?
7. The planet has experienced its hottest decade since 1880.
8. After the upheaval of the past ten days, the country has experienced a peaceful respite.

## DÉDALE

*Ce Collège d'Oxford est un véritable dédale.*[9] Masculine noun.

## DEFECTIVE VERBS

A defective verb is a verb that does not exist in all modes, at all tenses, or for all persons.

The following list is not exhaustive:

*Absoudre* (to absolve), *accroire* (to deceive), *apparoir* (to appear), *béer* (to be wide open), *bienvenir* (to be welcome), *braire* (to bray), *bruiner* (to drizzle), *chaloir* (to matter), *choir* (to fall), *clore* (to close), *ester* (to go to court), *falloir* (to need /have to), *faillir* (to very nearly … …), *férir* (without meeting any opposition), *frire* (to fry), *gésir* (to lie), *grêler* (to hail), *issir* (to leave), *messeoir* (to ill befit), *neiger* (to snow), *occire* (to slay), *oindre* (to anoint), *ouïr* (to hear), *paître* (to graze), *pleuvoir* (to rain), *poindre* (to come up), *pouvoir* (to be able to), *quérir* (to summon), *raire ou réer* (to bell[ow] /to troat [by a stag]), *ravoir* (to get back), *semondre* (to summon), *seoir* (to be proper to), *souloir* (to be used to), *tistre ou tître* (to weave), *traire* (to milk) – and its derivates:

*abstraire* (to abstract) *distraire* (to entertain) *extraire* (to extract) *soustraire* (to substract),

*transir* (to chill to the bone), *vouloir* (to want).

In this list, one can distinguish:

(a) Verbs that only conjugate with certain subject pronouns (*bruiner, neiger, pleuvoir, seoir, falloir…*). The verb *pleuvoir* is normally used in the third person singular but can be found in the third person plural (in the figurative sense): *les balles et les obus pleuvent.*

9. This Oxford College is a real labyrinth.

(b) Verbs that only conjugate in certains tenses or moods: *choir*, *clore*, *gésir*, *seoir*, *férir* etc.
(c) Verbs for which all the forms exist, but some are hardly known or used (*frire*, *paître*, *traire* etc.)
(d) Many verbs are archaic or very rare (*apparoir*, *souloir*, *semondre*).

It must be noted that *chaloir* is mostly used in the third person singular of the present indicative:

*Peu me chaut que ce soit l'exigence des Britanniques !*[10]

*Tistre*, *tître* [synonymous with *tisser* (to weave)] are only used as the past participle *tissu*, most often figuratively:

*Elle a tissu une toile.*[11]

## DÉGINGANDÉ

*Son allure dégingandée était très caractéristique.*[12]

The first *g* is *not* followed by a '*u*' and is pronounced like the *j* in *jardin* or *jadis*.

LE GÉNÉRAL

## DÉJEUNER

*Elle a pris son petit déjeuner à la terrasse d'un café à Marseille.*[13]

*Déjeuner* does not take a circumflex. The verb *petit-déjeuner* is hyphenated (and sometimes the noun *petit déjeuner* is joined with a hyphen).

In France: *le petit déjeuner* means 'breakfast',
*le déjeuner* means 'lunch', and *le dîner* means 'dinner';
while in Swiss French (as well as in francophone Quebec and Belgium): *le déjeuner* means 'breakfast',
*le dîner* means 'lunch', and *le souper* means 'dinner'.

## DÉLICE

*Il faut savoir apprécier les petites délices de la vie.*

*Délice* is masculine in the singular and feminine in the plural.

With *un de*, grammarians recommend the use of *délice* in the masculine: *Un de mes plus grands délices est d'écouter Mozart.*

See also AMOUR and ORGUE.

10 Little do I care that it is a demand of the British!
11. She wove a canvas.
12. He/she had a distinctive gangly appearance.
13. She had her breakfast on the terrace of a café in Marseille.

## DEMEURER

Which auxiliary does *demeurer* take?

—When it means 'to remain,' *demeurer* takes the auxiliary « *être* » :

*Il est demeuré impassible.*

—When it means 'to live,' *demeurer* takes the auxiliary « *avoir* » :

*Notre médecin de famille a demeuré à Salon de Provence pendant cette période.*[14]

Note: the verb is generally used without a preposition:

*Elle demeure avenue de la Brunante.*

However, we write *demeurer + au* when the address includes a digit not immediately followed by *rue*, *avenue*, etc.:

*Elle demeure au 14 de l'avenue de la Brunante.*

*/ Elle demeure 14 avenue de la Brunante.*

This type of specific complement of place simply permits the omission of the preposition (which has nothing to do with the verb itself, as it works with all verbs: *Elle habite avenue de la Brunante*, or *le film a été tourné avenue de la Brunante*, for example).

## DEMI

*Demi* is invariable when it comes before the noun it qualifies. When it follows the noun, it agrees for gender but not for number: *une demi-heure*, *deux heures et demie.*

## DÉMOCRATIE

*La Libye se prépare à la démocratie.*

Spelled with a '*t*' as derived from the Greek *democratia* (δημοκρατία), but pronounced with an /s/. The phoneme *-ti-* followed by a vowel is often pronounced /s/: cf. *nation, lotion.*

## DÉPENS (AUX –)

*Elle vit aux dépens de son frère.*[15]

Fixed expression which exists only in the plural:

*aux dépens de.*

14. Our family doctor stayed in Salon de Provence during that period.
15. She lives at the expense of her brother.

## DÉPEUPLER

*Tous ces endroits se sont dépeuplés de lions.*[16]

There is agreement here because it is not about just one lion. These locations are not empty of *a lion*, but of *lions*, plural.

## DES (Article)

(a) *Le texte nous fournit des interprétations différentes.*
(b) *Le texte nous fournit différentes interprétations.*

In sentence (a), *différent* means: 'which shows a difference', 'which is not the same': *C'est tout différent*: 'it's quite different' or 'it's another thing entirely'.

In sentence (b), *différent* (placed before the noun) is used without an article and means 'various', 'several': *Différentes personnes se sont présentées.*

## DESCENDRE

*J'ai descendu dans mon jardin*
*Pour y cueillir du romarin. ...*[17]

In the children's song *Gentil Coq'licot* ('Nice Poppy'), there is an archaic use of the auxiliary. It is not a question of poetic license. The verb *avoir* originally translated an action, as opposed to the verb *être* which expresses the result of this action. This is a nuance which got lost in contemporary French. Emile Littré also advocated *j'ai parti ce matin* in the case of intransitive verbs (the action) which is distinguishable from *je suis parti* (the result).

## DÉSORMAIS / DORÉNAVANT

*Désormais, je ne travaillerai pas le vendredi.*
*Il allait dorénavant travailler le samedi et le dimanche.*

*Désormais* signifies 'from now on' and is used with the present or future.

From an etymological and pragmatic point of view, *Dorénavant* ('From now on') comes from « *d'ores en avant* » = « *à partir de maintenant* » ('from now on' or 'from this point

16. There are no more lions in any of these areas.
17. I went down to my garden in order to pick some rosemary there.

forward'), therefore the point of reference is rather the present. Its usage is rarer and more literary today than *désormais.*

## DÈS QUE

*Dès qu'il eut terminé ses devoirs, il s'en alla faire la sieste.*[18]

*Dès que* is followed by the indicative. In this example the past anterior is in combination with a past historic.

## DESTIN / DESTINÉE

*Destin*: a force which controls events to come.

*Il a décidé de prendre son destin en main.*[19]

In Greek theatre, « *destin* » referred to a superior and implacable force that seemed to have mapped out all future events in advance.

The word *destinée* sometimes refers to *destin*, but it also frequently takes on a more extended, vivid sense. We speak about *destinée* when referring to the lives of great men and women, people who are special in some way and different from the majority: *La destinée de ce poète était toute tracée.*

## DEVOIR

The past participle of *devoir* takes a circumflex in the masculine singular, simply to distinguish it from the partitive article *du* : the forms are *dû*, *dus*, *due*, *dues.*

Compare:

*Il a dû partir* : he was obliged to leave.

*Il doit être parti* : I assume that he left, that he decided to leave. – The first formulation can also be employed with the meaning of the second.

ZOLA

## DIRE (Usages of)

Example 1:

« *Il disait Dienné, l'ancienne ville reine, au peuple, aux monuments venus d'Égypte, qui règne encore sur la vallée. Il disait... Il disait surtout Tombouctou... Il disait...* » (—Zola).

18. As soon as he had finished his homework, he went to have a nap.

19. He decided to take his fate into his own hands.

The verb *dire* has the sense of recounting, recalling, speaking about, and bringing things to life through speech and the written word. This is a rather literary usage which recalls the great epics: the French translation of Virgil's *Aeneid* begins: « *Je chante le héros et ses combats…* » (*'Arma virumque cano'* in Latin). The original Latin *cano* (« *je chante* ») stresses the musical form of the poem.

D'ORMESSON

EXAMPLE 2:

« *Un jour je m'en irai sans en avoir tout dit* » ('One Day I Will Go Away Without Having Said It All') is the title of a work by Jean D'Ormesson. It refers to a poem by Aragon. The anaphoric « *en* » of « *sans en avoir tout dit* » implies: « *sans avoir tout dit du monde* » ('without having said everything about the world'). The poem starts as follows:

> « *C'est une chose étrange à la fin que le monde*
> *Un jour je m'en irai sans en avoir tout dit*
> *Ces moments de bonheur ces midis d'incendie*
> *La nuit immense et noire aux déchirures blondes.* »[20]

« *Dire quelque chose* de *quelque chose* » = 'to say something *about* something', i.e. that which we were discussing, of the place we were discussing; in other words –

'… without having said it all about this world which is a strange thing in the end (*une chose étrange à la fin*), without having told of these happy times (*ces moments de bonheur*), these incendiary noons (*ces midis d'incendie*), the immense and black night with its blond tears (*la nuit immense et noire aux déchirures blondes*).'

*Il va sans dire / Il va s'en dire :*

« *Il va sans dire* » ('It goes without saying' = needless to say, without one saying it).

« *Il va s'en dire* » ('Things are going to be said'). It is a mistake to use this in the preceding sense. This expression

20. 'How strange the world is, in the end!
One day, I shall leave it without having said it all:
These happy moments, these ardent noons,
The immense night sky with its golden streaks.'

could be used in a sentence such as: « *Il va s'en dire des choses sur ce qui vient d'arriver* »[21] (many comments will be made; some things will be said).

## DISPARAÎTRE

*A cause de la chasse à outrance et d'une mauvaise adaptation à son environnement, le dodo a disparu.*[22]
*Mon collègue de bureau est disparu.*

In the first example, *disparaître* is used in the passé composé (*avoir*). The emphasis is on the action of disappearing. In the second, *disparu* used with *être* is used as an adjective to indicate a state.

*Disparaître* could mean to disappear or to be deceased depending on the context.

## DISSOUDRE

*Le sucre s'est dissous dans l'eau.*
*L'assemblée nationale a été dissoute.*

The past participle of *dissoudre* is *dissous* in the masculine and *dissoute* in the feminine. *Dissolu* means 'corrupted'.

## DIVIN

*Il est né le divin Enfant.*

Adjectives which end in a nasal vowel are denasalised when they are followed by a word beginning with a vowel which is pronounced: they are therefore pronounced in the same way as their feminine form. – *Un bon ami /une bonne amie.*

Note that the word *divin* is normally found *after* the noun rather than before it. The inversion makes it more poetic and literary.

## DOCTEUR

*J'ai rendez-vous chez le docteur.*

With a noun phrase referring to a person, we use the preposition *chez*.

21. Things are going to be said about what has just happened.
22. Due to excessive hunting and poor adaptation to its environment, the dodo disappeared.

## DOMINANCE / DOMINATION

*Les entrepreneurs exerçaient une certaine dominance sur le secteur privé.*
*La domination des grandes puissances vont s'accroître sensiblement.*

*Domination* is the act of dominating. It assumes that there is a dominator and a dominated.

*Dominance* refers to ascendancy, a superiority that appears as fact. It does not assume defeat or victim.

## DOM JUAN / DON JUAN

*Dom Juan est au programme du bac cette année.*

*Don Juan* refers to the character in Molière's play. However, in 17th-century French *Dom* was written for the Spanish *Don* and this spelling is preserved when referring to the play *Dom Juan.*

## DONT / DUQUEL / DE QUI

*L'homme duquel /dont /de qui je doute.*

*Duquel*, *dont* and *de qui* are all used, but with subtle differences of meaning –

*Duquel* implies that there is a choice (in the example, one of the men I am speaking of is the subject of my doubt).

*Dont* implies that I am speaking about someone and it is he/she I am referring to. This is the normal usage.

*De qui* (more colloquial) has the same sense as *dont* here but is only used for people, or personified things.

## D'ORES ET DÉJÀ

*Elle vous prévient d'ores et déjà qu'elle ne viendra pas.*[23]

*D'ores et déjà* is an emphatic variant of *déjà.* Its usage is literary.

## DORMIR

*Les heures qu'il a dormies ; les 3 heures qu'il a dormi.*

See Vivre.

23. She can already tell you that she will not come.

## DOUBLE COMPOUND TENSES

*Lorsqu'il a eu terminé de manger, il est allé se coucher.*

*Le passé surcomposé* is used in colloquial French. It is considered as the oral form of the past anterior, especially used in the South of France, Quebec, and Switzerland. As Professor Louis de Saussure in Neuchâtel told us: 'In the Francophone domain (Switzerland, Languedoc, Provence etc), the double compound past is very productive and very common, without giving the impression of being particularly familiar, as in « *J'ai eu aimé aller au cinéma.* »[24] ' (private communication, January 2014).

One can find a good number of examples in literature of the *passé surcomposé* (double compound past) associated with the literary register, but these usages are outdated today. In these constructions, a double compound past associated with a perfect tense replaces a past anterior associated with a simple past:

(a) It can be found just like the past anterior, after a temporal subordinating conjunction expressing anteriority or simultaneity:

« *Après qu'ils ont eu causé un instant en tête-à-tête…la duchesse lui a dit…* »
(—Dumas, cited by Damourette & Pichon 1911-1936, V, 294).[25]

« *Quand la France a eu réalisé son programme révolutionnaire, elle a découvert à la Révolution toute espèce de défauts…* »
(—Renan, cited by Grevisse and Goosse: 1993, p1190).[26]

ALEXANDRE DUMAS PÈRE

(b) It can be found just like the past anterior in an independent clause with an adverb expressing a delay in the accomplishment of the process:

24. I had loved going to the cinema.

25. After having spoken one-on-one for an instant, the duchess told him…

26. When France had achieved its revolutionary programme, it discovered all kinds of problems during the Revolution.

« *Ce petit vin nouveau … a eu vite grisé tous ces buveurs de bière* » (—Daudet, cited by Grevisse and Goosse: 1993, 1190).[27]

« *À peine avons-nous eu dîné que mon mari a proposé une promenade* » (—S. Cottin, cited by Imbs: 1960, 133).[28]

« *Il a fallu la relever [l'automobile]. À une heure du matin, nous avons eu fini* » (—Damourette & Pichon : 1911-1936, V, 298).[29]

—These sentences intend to mark anteriority within anteriority, but if the principal is in the perfect tense, the perfect of the subordinate does not do justice to this expressive need. The solution that should logically be imposed is that of the double compound past as in these examples. It remains that this formulation is somewhat familiar today to Francophones.

We also find, although these usages are less frequent: the *passé antérieur surcomposé* (*j'eus été parti*), the *plus-que-parfait surcomposé* (*j'avais été envoyé*) and the *conditionnel passé surcomposé* (*j'aurais été parti*) attested by the Bescherelle (1997), but their usage is extremely rare.

In French-speaking Switzerland, one says « *Il est eu parti* » instead of « *Il a été parti* ».

[Historically, the origin of *le passé surcomposé* can be traced back to the 15th century or even earlier: 'According to Pfister (1974: 415), the PSC would have spread in the 15th century to express an accomplished action. De Vogel (1955: 59) also finds his earliest examples at that time in Eastern France, but Foulet (1925: 208) claims that the verbal form must have been found in oral language prior to that time, and suggests it emerged during the 13th century even though if, in theory, PSC would have been possible since Romance compound forms first emerged (Sneyders de Vogel 1955: 62); —from Labeau's *Chronicle of a Death Foretold: the French Simple Past* (in preparation).]

27. This new little wine…had quickly intoxicated all these beer drinkers.

28. We had barely had dinner when my husband proposed taking a walk.

29. It was necessary to lift it [the automobile] up. At one o'clock in the morning, we had finished.

## DOUBLE HYPHEN

According to a 2004 circular, a double hyphen should separate, on the civil status certificates, the names of children who possess the family name of both their parents (such as Dupont--François, for example). In 2010, the double hyphen was invalidated by the State Council.

## DRÔLE

*Il se passe de drôles de choses dans cette école.*

As in this example, there is an '-*s*' on *drôles*, as it functions adjectivally.

## DUPE

*L'esprit est toujours la dupe du cœur.*

The noun *dupe* is feminine: *une dupe*. The adjective agrees in gender and number.

## DUSSÉ-JE

First-person singular of the imperfect subjunctive of the verb *devoir*. The final '*e*' has an acute accent but is pronounced as a grave (like « *puissé-je* », « *eussé-je* »). The expression, which means 'even if I should,' is literary in register.

*Je préférerais me battre, dussé-je y perdre la vie.*[30]

30. I would prefer to fight, even to the death.

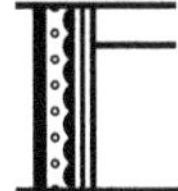

## E (Pronunciation of)

Clemenceau

The proper nouns Clemenceau, Grevisse, Mitterrand, and Trenet are written without an acute accent, and the '*e*' is pronounced /ə/; but in common usage the 'e' is pronounced as if accented, i.e. « Cl*é*menceau ».

## ÉCARLATE

*Leurs visages écarlates respiraient le bonheur.*[1]

Colour adjective deriving from a noun, but one of the exceptions and therefore agreeing normally with the verb.

See Amarante, Fauve, Incarnat, Mauve, Pourpre, and Rose.

## ÉCHAPPATOIRE

*La littérature est pour lui une échappatoire.*[2] Feminine noun.

## ÉCHAPPER / S'ÉCHAPPER

*Échapper :* to leave, by ruse, or by force, someone that was holding, retaining, guarding: *le voleur a échappé à la police.*

Not to be reached by someone, something; to evade; to avoid:
*Échapper à une sanction.*

Not to be obtained by someone: *Le gros lot lui a échappé.*

To pull away from, to detach from someone:
*Je sens qu'il m'échappe, il doit avoir d'autres intérêts ailleurs.*

Not to be perceived, grasped, understood, retained by someone:
*Son nom m'échappe.*

To accidentally fall from the hands (+ *avoir*):
*Les assiettes lui ont échappé des mains.*

To let slip inadvertently (+ *être*): *Un mot de regret lui est échappé.*

*S'échapper* : To exit a location, to escape it, to leave it by ruse or by force: *le tigre s'est échappé du zoo.*

1. Their scarlet faces exuded happiness.
2. Literature is a form of escapism for him.

To discreetly leave a meeting, a reunion; to slip away /to slip out, to steal away:

*Elle s'est échappée après le repas.*

To gush, to come out of something, of a place:

*L'eau s'échappe du tuyau percé.*

To dissipate, to faint, to fall, to leave:

*Il a vu s'échapper son dernier espoir de victoire.*

When speaking of one or more runners, to outpace the other competitors:

*Le cycliste s'est échappé du peloton.*

## ÉCHO

*Ces vers de Rimbaud se sont fait l'écho de ses angoisses.*[3]

The past participle *fait* is always invariable in the expression *se faire l'écho de.*

See Faire.

## ÉCLAIR

*J'ai fait une visite éclair dans la ville de Dijon.*[4]

The noun *éclair* used with another noun is invariable: *Des attaques éclair, une campagne éclair, une guerre éclair, une offensive éclair, une opération éclair, un passage éclair, un raid éclair…*

## ÉCRIVAIN / ÉCRIVAINE

*Françoise Sagan est un célèbre écrivain français /une célèbre écrivaine française.*

The adjective will agree with the subject. In Canada, *écrivaine* is now more usual. Elsewhere, the feminine form is not common. In Switzerland titles are feminized more than in France.

Sagan

The forms *une jeune écrivaine* and *madame le professeur* (as opposed to the more formal *madame la professeure*) are commonly used in everyday French.

3. These verses by Rimbaud echoed his anguish.
4. I made a quick visit to Dijon. [I made a lighting-fast visit to Dijon.]

## ÉGLISE

*La cérémonie eut lieu en l'Église Saint-Sulpice.*

The construction *en l'église* is commonly found when it is accompanied by a proper noun. It is a more formal variant of *à l'église*.

## ÉLAN / ÉLAND

The word *élan* denotes a large deer or moose from Scandinavia, Siberia, the USA and Canada:

*L'élan est un animal indépendant et solitaire.*[5]

*The éland* is a large African antelope:

*L'éland est un animal diurne.*[6]

## EMPORTER

*En français, le masculin l'emporte sur le féminin.*[7]

The neuter *le* appears in many expressions in French, and has no specific grammatical function, as in: *le disputer à*, *l'emporter sur*, *le prendre de haut*.

One also finds the object pronoun *la* in certain idiomatic expressions: « *Se la couler douce* » ; « *la* » here replaces the implicit noun « *la vie* » or « *l'existence* » (= 'to take it easy' / 'to enjoy an easy life').

## EN

Example 1: *Elles en ont mangé, des coings.*[8]

The past participle does not agree with the neuter collective pronoun *en*.

Example 2: *Des maisons, elles s'en sont construit.*

Again, the past participle does not agree with the neuter collective pronoun *en*.

Example 3: *Allez-vous-en ; rendez-vous-y.*

When two pronouns come together and one of them is *y* or *en*, the *y* or *en* comes last.

5. The elk/moose is a solitary and independent animal.
6. Antelopes are diurnal animals.
7. In French, the masculine prevails over the feminine.
8. They have eaten many quinces. ['Of quinces, they have eaten many' (cleft object).]

Example 4: *Les leçons que j'en ai tirées étaient inestimables.*[9]

In this sentence, *que*, replacing *les leçons*, is the preceding direct object and *en* is the indirect object standing implicitly for *de cette expérience.*

## ENCORE / TOUJOURS

*Il est encore là /il est toujours là.*

These are broadly synonymous, but depending on the intonation, the latter can have a negative connotation implying 'he is here again' rather than 'he is still here.' *Toujours* expresses permanence and temporal continuity, while *encore* can be used in different contexts with different meanings, according to the structure of the phrase (*pas encore, encore une fois, encore que, si encore…*).

*Encor* is an archaic poetic form: « *Et la raison encor ne m'en est pas connue* » (—Molière, *L'École des femmes*, 1.4).

Molière

## ENNUYANT / ENNUYEUX

*Il est ennuyant avec ses histoires abracadabrantes.*[10]

*On supporte mal un conférencier ennuyeux.*[11]

*Ennuyant* is the present participle of the verb *ennuyer* and means *qui cause l'ennui.*

In Canada, the adjective *ennuyant* can mean: 'boring' /'tedious' /'wearisome.'

*Ennuyeux* (standard French) means 'slightly inconvenient or annoying' (*une affaire ennuyeuse*), and 'tiring,' 'boring,' 'monotonous': *un film /un travail ennuyeux* ; *des professeurs ennuyeux.*

9. The lessons that I learned [from it] were invaluable.
10. He is tiresome, with his far-fetched stories.
11. A boring speaker is insufferable.

## ENTRECÔTE

*Elle a mangé une entrecôte bien tendre dans l'un des meilleurs restaurants de Paris.*[12]

Until the 1920s, the word *entrecôte* was masculine, as witnessed by its use in *Le Grand Larousse du XX*eme *siècle* (1932), and it then became feminine probably due to the analogy between *une entrecôte* 'rib steak' and *une côte* 'rib' (feminine).

## ENTRE QUATRE YEUX

*Il lui dit la vérité entre quatre yeux.*[13]

There is no 's' on *quatre*, to avoid a false liaison.

## ENVI (À L')

*Ils ont dénoncé les abus des politiciens à l'envi.*[14]

Has no final 'e'. The expression means 'over and over again'.

## EPITHÈTE

*Une épithète est utilisée pour qualifier le nom.*[15]

Feminine noun.

## ÉQUINOXE

*C'est en plein équinoxe que nous irons nous promener près de la rivière.*

*Équinoxe* is masculine.

## ESPÈCE

*Cette espèce d'individu est dangereux.*

*L'inspecteur Maigret recherche une espèce d'individu dangereux /déséquilibré.*

*Espèce* is feminine. The adjective or past participle agrees with the preceding noun and not with the word *espèce*.

MAIGRET
[JEAN GABIN]

12. She ate a very tender rib steak in one of the best restaurants in Paris.
13. He told [him/her] the truth face-to-face.
14. They denounced the politicians' misdeeds at every possible opportunity.
15. An attributive adjective is used to qualify the noun.

## ESPÉRER

When it is affirmative, the verb is in the indicative or the conditional if followed with a *si* clause:

*J'espère qu'il comprendra. Elle espère qu'il lui dirait* [*conditionnel*] *si elle se trompait* [*imparfait*].

When it is negative, it takes the subjunctive:

*Je n'espère plus qu'il me rejoigne.*

When it is interrogative, both the indicative and the subjunctive are acceptable: *Espères-tu qu'il viendra /vienne ?*

It seems that with time the verb *espérer* has been increasingly perceived as a verb of 'desire,' of 'wish,' and verbs of this group require the subjunctive.

## ESPOIR / ESPÉRANCE

*Tant qu'il y a de la vie, il y a de l'espoir.*[16]

*Nous nourrissons de folles espérances qu'elle revienne au pays.*[17]

*L'espoir* (hope) is the simple desire that something goes or ends well.

*L'espérance* (expectation) contains the idea of trust or certitude. The term has more of a religious or solemn sense.

## ESSENTIEL

*La motivation et la persévérance sont essentielles à sa réussite.*[18]

*Essentiels* in the masculine plural, and *essentielles* in the feminine plural.

## ESTHÉTIQUE

*Les films de Peter Greenaway sont d'une beauté esthétique qui rappelle celle d'une œuvre picturale.*[19]

*L'esthétique est considérée comme une philosophie.*

Can be used as an adjective or a noun. No accent on the initial *'e'*.

GREENAWAY

16. Where there is life, there is hope.
17. We are clinging to wild hopes that she returns to the country.
18. Motivation and perseverance are key to [his/her] success.
19. The aesthetic beauty of Peter Greenaway's films ressembles that of a painting.

## ET (Conjunction)

*Nous avons fait des recherches sur les origines graphique et fonctionnelle de la cédille en français.*[20]

Such a formulation avoids repeating the original word and gives the impression of a greater concision.

If we take a concrete example: Someone has two employees, one Italian and the other Spanish: we speak of *ses employés italien et espagnol* (his Italian and Spanish employees). We can, however, say *son employé italien et son employé espagnol* (his Italian employee and his Spanish employee).

The redundance of the coordinating conjunction *et* 'and' (polysyndeton) is very common before an adjective. It is a form of emphasis: *Ils sont et intelligents et travailleurs.*

## ÉTATSUNIEN

*Les élections étatsuniennes auront lieu en fin de semaine prochaine.*

All of the following forms are found: *étatsunien*, *étasunien*, and *états-unien*. This is only found in relation to the United States of America.

As *America* denotes the whole continent, this word is sometimes used, but in reality, *américain* is more common.

In francophone Canada – unlike in France – speakers avoid using the word « *Amérique* » to designate the United States specifically. Although it is true that French speakers prefer using the adjective *américain* to *étatsunien*, they (at least if they are from a cultivated background) would generally use *États-Unis* rather than *Amérique*; especially in newspapers when talking about politics.

## ÉTONNER / S'ÉTONNER

*Il s'étonne de sa réussite / il est étonné de sa réussite.*

The difference in meaning is very slight. The first marks the beginning of the process. The second is a passive form and marks the state. For other verbs, the difference between the process and the state is very clear: *Madame se meurt* (= she is about to die) vs. *Madame est morte* (= she is dead).

20. We did research on the graphic and functional origins of the cedilla in French.

## EURO

*Il vous en coûtera quinze euros pour ce livre.*

The word *euro* is variable and takes an '–*s*' in the plural.

## ÉVÈNEMENT

Depardieu

*Le dernier film avec Depardieu c'est l'événement de la rentrée.*[21]

In the 16th century, the grave accent was not yet used on the vowel '*e*'. Robert Estienne was first to use the acute accent to create more visibility in his 1530 dictionary.

The written form *événement* with both accents acute is the form recommended by purists. Orthographers suggested the form *évènement* with a grave accent, in accordance with the pronunciation, because it is followed by a mute *e*. The *Académie Française*, in the ninth edition of its *Dictionnaire* and in accordance with the recommendations of the *Conseil supérieur de la langue française* in 1990, used the written form *évènement*, which is very common. As Foata and Fusch explain in their book *Calcul des probabilités* :

> « *La graphie avec l'accent aigu sur le 'e' de la deuxième syllabe n'a de justification ni phonétique, ni étymologique. Elle vient du fait qu'au XVII^e siècle on n'utilisait l'accent grave que sur le 'a' ou sur le 'u'. Quand pour la troisième édition (1740) on décida de mettre un accent grave sur des mots comme 'père', 'funèbre', 'allègre', etc…, l'imprimeur de l'Académie n'avait pas fondu assez de 'e' avec accent grave. Dans de nombreuses pages, il ne mit que des 'e' avec accent aigu.* »[22]

21. The latest film with Depardieu is the event of the start of the year.

22. "The '*e*' with an acute accent on the second syllable is not justifiable phonetically or etymologically. It comes from the fact that during the 17th century, one used the grave accent only on the '*a*' or the '*u*.' When for the third edition (1740) they decided to put a grave accent on words such as « *père* » ['father'], « *funèbre* » ['funereal'], « *allègre* » ['joyful'], etc…, the printer of the Academy had not made enough of the '*è*' with the grave accent. On many pages, he only put the '*é*' with the acute accent." [Quoted at http://www.bibmath.net/dico/index.php3?action=affiche&quoi=./l/langproba.html]

From that point on, dictionaries allowed both spellings, *événement* and *évènement.*

**EXAUCER / EXHAUSSER**

*Exaucer* means 'fulfil', 'grant someone's wish'.
*Exhausser* means 'raise the height of something', 'increase'.

*Ses désirs ont été exaucés.*
*Le mur a été exhaussé.*

**EXCLURE**

The past participle forms of *exclure* are *exclu / exclue* with no '–*s*', but those of *inclure* should be *inclus / incluse.*

*Sa nomination n'est pas exclue.*
*Sa lettre de candidature est-elle incluse dans le dossier ?*

Until the 18th century, the spellings *exclus* and *excluse* were accepted. In *Le Dictionnaire de l'Académie* from 1835 (sixth edition), the new spelling *exclu* replaced the previous one with the '*s*'. *Le Dictionnaire de l'Académie* from 1798 (fifth edition) was in the process of modernization, and we can imagine that the past participle of *exclure* was then modeled on that of *conclure.*

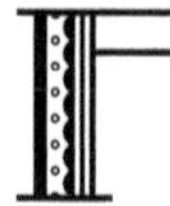

## FAÇON

*Elle ira à la piscine de toutes façons /de toute façon.*

The phrase *de toutes façons* (and also *de toute manière /en tout cas*) means 'whatever happens', 'in any way possible', and is the equivalent of 'anyway' in English.

## FAINÉANT

*Il ne travaille jamais, c'est un fainéant !*[1]

The spelling *feignant* is considered non-standard.

## FAIRE + INFINITIVE

The verb *faire* followed by an infinitive is invariable because it is considered to join with the infinitive to take on a passive sense.

*Ils se sont fait couper les cheveux.*

*Ils se sont fait licencier.*

Note: there is a subtle difference between *Paul a été blessé* and *Paul s'est fait blesser.* – In the former, someone injured Paul. In the latter, Paul was put in a situation in which he was injured.

## FAIRE TOMBER / LAISSER TOMBER

*Elle a fait tomber un vase en porcelaine.*[2]

*Elle a laissé tomber un mouchoir.*[3]

*Faire tomber* is an involuntary action.

*Laisser tomber* is a voluntary action.

1. He never works, he's a layabout!
2. She knocked over a china vase.
3. She dropped her handkerchief.

## FAIT

*Il a été mis devant le fait accompli.*

Normally, the final *'t'* in the noun *fait* is not pronounced. It is the French media that popularized the pronunciation of the *'t'* in *fait* like that of *août.*

Some people pronounce the *'t'* in the singular, but not the plural. We often hear it pronounced in the expression *en fait* and several other expressions like *malgré le fait que.*

## FAÎTE

*Il est monté jusqu'au faîte du Snowdon.*

*Faîte*, meaning a 'mountain peak', has a circumflex.

## FALLOIR

*Je ne crois pas qu'il faille toujours être d'accord avec ce qu'ils pensent.*[4]

*Falloir* can be used with an infinitive construction (more formal) or the subjunctive. Because it is an impersonal verb, *falloir* does not conjugate but the pronoun comes before: *il faut que je parte / il me faut partir.*

## FAUVE

Colour adjective derived from a noun, but one of the exceptions which therefore agrees normally: *des manteaux fauves.*

See Amarante, Écarlate, Incarnat, Mauve, Pourpre, and Rose

## FATIGANT / FATIGUANT

*J'ai trouvé ce voyage en avion très fatigant.*

*Ce n'est pas en te fatiguant devant l'écran que tu vas pouvoir récupérer de ta dure journée.*[5]

*Fatigant* is the adjective and *fatiguant* the present participle.

4. I do not believe that one must always agree with what they think.

5. Exhausting yourself in front of a screen will not help you to recover from a hard day.

## FEMINIZATION

The feminization of certain nouns is a subject of debate. Usage varies and we often find:

*Colette était une autrice /auteure*[6] */écrivaine fascinée par les chats.*[7]

or

*Colette était un auteur /écrivain fasciné par les chats.*

COLETTE

## FESTIVAL

*J'ai assisté à de nombreux festivals de cinéma au Canada.*

*Festival* becomes *festivals* in the plural.

## FEU

*Feu la reine / la feue reine.*[8]

The adjective *feu*, which is rare today, is unusual in being invariable when it is placed *before* the article and noun, and variable when it is placed *between* the article and the noun.

This expression has nothing to do with *le feu* ('fire'). It is, rather, a throwback to forms of the verb *'être'* in the *passé simple* : *feu mon père = fut mon père.*

## FIER (SE)

*Elle s'est fiée à son instinct.*

The verb *'se fier'* is essentially pronominal. The past particle agrees with the subject.

## FILS

*Je le considère comme mon fils.*

Why is the *'s'* of *'fils'* pronounced?

—It is probably because of its Latin origin (*filius*) or to distinguish it from the plural of *fil*, which means 'thread'.

6. Use of *'auteure'* rather than *'autrice'* is considered controversial.
7. Colette was a (female) author /authoress /writer who was fascinated by cats.
8. The late queen.

## FINNOIS / FINLANDAIS

*Le finnois est une langue fort difficile à apprendre.*

*Finnois :* A member of a people living mainly in Finland.

*Le finnois :* Finno-Ugric language spoken mainly in Finland, where it has official status, and in neighbouring regions.

*Finlandais :* A person born or living in Finland.

*Le finlandais :* Synonymous with *le finnois*, the language spoken in Finland.

Some people prefer the word *finnois* because there are Finnish people who speak Swedish as their native language. Finnish is not their language, despite the fact that they are Finnish by nationality.

## FLAGADA

*Ils se sentent tout flagada.*[9]

*Flagada* is invariable. *Le Flagada* is originally a comic strip that appeared in the newspaper *Spirou* in 1961.

## FLAMBANT NEUF

There are normally two possible patterns of agreement:

*Des voitures flambant neuves*[10] (the most frequent pattern – *flambant* is considered as a present participle and remains invariable); and

*Des voitures flambant neuf* (both words invariable).

## FLÛTE

« *Flûte, je ne sais plus jouer de la flûte* » *dit-il en riant.*[11]

Written with a circumflex.

The Provençale word from which *flûte* (the instrument) derives was written *flaüt* and appeared in the 13th century in the forms *fleuste*, *fluste*. The circumflex accent replaces the missing 's'. The interjection, which appears much later (from 1858), expresses disappointment.

9. They feel completely wiped out.
10. Brand-new cars.
11. 'Shoot, I can no longer play the flute!' he said laughing.

## FOI / FOIE

*Il était une fois,*
*Dans la ville de Foix,*
*Une marchande de foie,*
*Qui vendait du foie…*
*Elle se dit : Ma foi,*
*C'est la première fois*
*Et la dernière fois,*
*Que je vends du foie,*
*Dans la ville de Foix.*

This mnemonic nursery rhyme contains the four homophones: *foi* (faith), *foie* (liver), *fois* (time), and *Foix* (French town and commune in the Ariège Department).

## FOLIES BERGÈRE

*J'ai assisté à un spectacle de danse aux Folies Bergère.*

*Folies Bergère* is written without an 's' on *Bergère* because it refers to the Music Hall *Les Folies* in the nearby *rue Bergère* and not *folies* of several *bergères.*

## FOND / FONDS

*Il a un bon fonds.*[12] */La maison se trouve au fond du jardin.*[13]

When referring to physical, moral, or intellectual qualities, *fonds* is written with an 's' (although *avoir un bon fond* is also correct according to the *TLF*). We also speak of *fonds de commerce* (a group of assets/holdings).

## FOURMI

*[La cigale] alla crier famine chez la fourmi sa voisine*[14] (—La Fontaine, *La Cigale et la fourmi*).

*Fourmi* was masculine until the 16th century. The spelling, without a final '*–e*', corresponds to the old masculine form of this word.

LA FONTAINE

12. He has a good character
13. The house is located at the end of the garden.
14. [The cicada] went to plea her hunger to her neighbour the ant.

**FUTURE / CONDITIONAL**

*Paul a dit qu'il viendra. /Paul a dit qu'il viendrait.*

Both sentences are acceptable. There is a stylistic difference, with the second sentence being more literary in register. The first is often heard in conversation.

*Paul a dit qu'il viendra :* he will come at a time later than the utterance of the sentence. For example, imagine it is currently Tuesday – the meeting will take place on Thursday, and this sentence is in response to someone asking if Paul will be there.

*Paul a dit qu'il viendrait :* Paul will come after the time at which *he* spoke. Paul's words in direct speech were 'I will be at the meeting.' The sequence of tense agreement is here carried out.

## GAME BOY

*On lui a acheté une gameboy (/un game boy) pour son anniversaire.*

Both *le* and *la* are used, although the company Nintendo objects to the use of the feminine gender. It is very often feminine, from « *la (console de)…* ».

## GÂTEAU

*Je n'ai jamais goûté au gâteau de ta grand-mère.*

The circumflex on the *'a'* of *gâteau* marks the loss of an *'s'* (in the 13th century, the word was written *gastiau*). *Gâteau* is invariable when used adjectivally: *ce sont de vrais papas gâteau.*[1]

## GENDER

(a) The main words that change meaning according to gender are:

| *un aigle* (an eagle) | *une aigle* (an eagle on a flag/crest) |
|---|---|
| *un barbe* (a barb) | *une barbe* (a beard) |
| *un critique* (a critic) | *une critique* (a criticism, or a review) |
| *un faune* (a faun) | *une faune* (a fauna) |
| *un garde* (a guard) | *une garde* (the soldier's guard, e.g. in front of a building) |
| *un gîte* (a form, the hare's burrow, a holiday cottage) | |
| | *une gîte* (according to *TLF*, a navy term to designate the location where a ship that has run aground is lodged) |
| *un greffe* (a court's administration), | |
| | *une greffe* (a graft/transplant) |
| *un hymne* (an anthem) | *une hymne* (a religious hymn) |
| *un litre* (a litre) | *une litre* (a black funerary border) |
| *un livre* (a book) | *une livre* (a pound weight/sterling) |
| *un manche* (a handle) | *une manche* (a half /round of a game, a sleeve) |
| *un moule* (a mould) | *une moule* (a mussel) |

1. They are real softies.

*un mousse* (a ship's boy) *la mousse* (froth)
*un ombre* (a grayling, a type of large fish)
*une ombre* (a shade)
*un page* (a page /squire) *une page* (a page in a book)
*un paillasse* (a clown) *une paillasse* (a straw mattress)
*un parallèle* (line of latitude) *une parallèle* (a parallel)
*un pendule* (a pendulum) *une pendule* (a clock)
*le platine* (platinum) *une platine* (a turn table)
*un somme* (a nap) *une somme* (a sum)
*un tour* (a turning machine /lathe /a walk: *je vais faire un tour*[2] /*Le Tour de France*) *une tour* (a tower)
*un vase* (a vase) *la vase* (mud /sludge)
*un vapeur* (a steamboat) *une vapeur* (a steam)
*un voile* (a veil) *une voile* (a sail)

(b) The most common words with double gender (both maculine and feminine):
*aprèm* (afternoon) *après-guerre* (postwar years)
*après-midi* (afternoon) *chistéra* (wicker basket in game of pelota)
*clope* (cig, butt) *enzyme* (enzyme)
*goulache /goulasch* (goulash) *H.L.M./HLM* (council house /estate)[3]
*ordonnance* (prescription) *parka* (a parka)
*perce-neige* ( a snowdrop) *phalène* (geometrid moth)
*poiscaille* (derogatory term for fish)
*radio-trottoir* (gossip / street interview /word of mouth)
*sitcom* (sitcom) *synopsis* (synopsis)
*teuf-teuf* (puff-puff /chuff-chuff /old car /jalopy).

(c) Are there rules for establishing the gender of nouns?

—Nouns which end in *–e*, *–tion*, *–té*, and *–ance* are usually feminine.

A general rule is that nouns tend to have the same gender they had in Latin, with the Latin neuter becoming masculine in French. However, the words from the third declension are much more tricky: cf. *flos, floris* (masculine in Latin) which becomes *la fleur* (feminine).

2. I am going to take a walk
3. *Habitation à loyer modéré* (*/modique* in Québec).

Nouns ending in *-tion* come from Latin nouns ending in *–tio*(*nis*), which are feminine.

Nouns ending in *–é*, which come from Latin nouns ending in *–ia*, are feminine, as are nouns ending in *–té*, which come from Latin nouns ending in *–tas*, *–tatis*, e.g. *charité* (*caritas*, *caritatis*).

The noun *fleuve* (ending in *–e*) comes from the masculine *fluvius*, and *globe* comes from *globus*, also masculine.

(d) Nouns to note:

Masculine:

*agrume*, *amalgame*, *antidote*, *antipode*,
*aparté*, *aphte*, *apogée*, *are*,
*astérisque*, *augure*, *cèpe*, *effluve*,
*éloge*, *emblème*, *en-tête*, *entracte*,
*équinoxe*, *exode*, *interstice*, *intervalle*,
*méandre*, *média*, *obélisque*, *opuscule*,
*pastiche*, *pénates*, *pétale*, *planisphère*,
*rail*, *tentacule*.

Feminine:

*acné*, *agrafe*, *alluvion*, *amnistie*,
*anagramme*, *apostrophe*, *atmosphère*, *échappatoire*,
*écritoire*, *éliminatoires*, *éphéméride*, *épithète*,
*épître*, *équivoque*, *giboulée*, *icône*,
*idylle*, *immondices*, *interview*, *mandibule*,
*nacre*, *octave*, *omoplate*, *orbite*,
*volte-face*.

See also MASCULINE/FEMININE.

## GENDER (BRAND)

*Il a commandé une Vittel /un Perrier.*

As a general rule, the gender of a brand reflects that of the product. Basically, *une Evian*, *une Badoit*, *une Volvic*, etc., are said, because they are types of water (*une eau* in French), but it is also linked to the source of the water (*une source* which is feminine in French): 'water from the thermal town /springs of …'

For Perrier, the use of *'un'* is truly a commercial choice. In the 1990s, for example, there was a slogan that bragged about *la violence d'un Perrier* (the violence of a Perrier). Apparently the brand wanted to distinguish itself from its competitors by its strong sparkle: here, the masculine is justified, because it is associated with strength, violence, energy, etc.

*Un Vittel fraise* (shortened from a *'Vittel fraise apéritif'*) is used.

Similarly, nearly all car brands are feminine. Therefore *une Peugeot*, *une Renault*, *une Citroën* etc., are used. But sometimes brand advertising strategies change this usage. One advertisement spoke of *le nouveau Renault Captur*. Here it is really a deliberate choice (maybe the masculine gives an image of dependability, of strength?).

UNE 2CV

## GENS

*Les vieilles gens sont de plus en nombreuses dans cette ville.*

Feminine noun when the adjective is preceding, but the adjective remains in the masculine when it follows: *les gens sont nombreux*. Originally, *gens* was the plural of *gent*.

## GENT

*La gent*[4] *féminine ne le laisse jamais indifférent.*

Feminine noun.

## GENTIMENT

*Il s'est comporté gentiment.*

Adverb formed from the adjective gentil.

## GÉORGIE

*La Géorgie est située aux confins de l'Europe et de l'Asie.*

*Géorgie* comes from the Greek γεωργία 'agriculture' (literally 'the work on earth': γῆ (earth) + ἔργον (work). The name 'George' has the same origin and means 'agriculture'.

One pronounces the American state of *Géorgie* as /jorji/.

4. '–kind' (as in 'womankind', 'mankind').

## GEORGIEN / GÉORGIEN

*Des meubles georgiens.*

Refers to the Georgian style of furniture, as opposed to '...*géorgiens*' ('from Georgia').

## GIBOULÉE

*Les premières giboulées de mars viennent de tomber.*[5]

Feminine noun.

## GISANT

*Dans la chapelle illuminée, on pouvait apercevoir le gisant du roi Edouard.*[6]

Present participle of the verb *gésir* used as a noun. *Un gisant* is a statue representing someone lying down ('a recumbent statue'). This very infrequent verb is especially found on epitaphs: *Ci-gît un brave*... ('Here lies...') with a circumflex.

## GOULÛMENT

*Elles mangeaient goulûment les bonnes crêpes préparées par leur mamie.*[7]

Adjectives ending in '–*u*' take a circumflex when they become adverbs: *continûment*.

## GOÛTER

*Il goûte à une pomme /Il goûte une pomme.*

To mean eating a small amount of something to discover its taste (e.g. a taste one is not familiar with), we use *goûter à*.

*Goûte à ça* = try this /have a taste of this.

*Goûte ça* = appreciate the taste of this /savour this.

## GOUTTE

*Je n'y vois goutte.*[8]

The expression *ne...goutte* is very archaic and also used in colloquial language.

5. The first hail showers of March have just fallen.
6. The recumbent statue of King Edward could be glimpsed in the lit chapel.
7. They greedily gobbled down the delicious crepes that their granny had made.
8. I cannot see a thing.

Expressions such as *je ne vois point ; je ne bois goutte ; je ne mange mie ; je ne marche pas* come from Medieval French and are rated literary today. Originally, there would only be the negation *ne. Pas* comes from literally 'a step' (*un pas*) in the phrase *je ne marche pas.*

## GOUVERNANCE / GOUVERNEMENT

*Les chefs d'État ont formulé des propositions concrètes pour améliorer la gouvernance de l'espace européen.*[9]
*Le gouvernement zambien s'est attaqué à la pauvreté.*

*Gouvernance* is the way of and the manner of administrating, not only of governing. It is also the group of rules that must be observed. We can speak of good and bad governance.

*Gouvernement* is the authority of the State and of what resembles it as an organization.

## GRAND

*Il dormait les yeux grands ouverts.*

The adjective *grand* in the expression *grand ouvert* agrees in gender and number with the adjective *ouvert* which follows it.

## GRAND-MÈRE

The plural is *grands-mères.* However, general dictionaries are not unanimous when it comes to the '*s*' of '*grands*'.

*Grand'mère* is an older spelling. The apostrophe is there to replace the *e* which would normally be present in the feminine form of *grand. Mère-grand* was used in the 15th century. This word is found in the fairy-tale: *Le Conte de la mère-grand.*

Originally, the Latin adjective and its derivates were invariable. In the 16th century, the '*e*' was added to the feminine form. The original invariable adjectival form remains in fixed expressions such as *grand-mère.* So that *grand* is not mistaken for a qualification of *mère* (i.e. a mother who is large /tall), *grand* takes the masculine form. *Grand-messe* is not the opposite of *petite-messe*, but of *basse-messe* or *messe basse.* Similarly, one would write *à grand-peine.*

9. The Heads of State have put forward concrete proposals to improve the governance of the European area.

## GRAND-PARENT

*Chaque été je vais voir mes grands-parents à la campagne.*

The plural form is *grands-parents.*

## GRAND-PEINE

*Il a réussi à grand-peine.*

*Grand* is an adverb, and therefore invariable.

## GREC / GRECQUE

*Nous contemplions de magnifiques amphores grecques.*[10]

The feminine form, ending in *–cque*, is quite different from the masculine.

Adjectives ending in *'c'* have their feminine form in *'che'* (*sec /sèche*) or in *'que'* (*turc /turque*) according to each case. The feminine of *'grec'* is *'grecque'* for the sake of pronunciation. Doubling the consonant, as is usually done in the French feminine form (such as *bon /bonne*, *cruel /cruelle*, etc.), would have led to writing *'grecce'*, therefore, to preserve the /k/ sound of the masculine in front of *'e'*, the *'c'* becomes *'–qu'*, which is the reason for *'grecque'*.

## GROENLAND

*Cet aventurier a commencé une expédition au Groenland.*[11]

The word does not take a diaeresis. It comes from the Scandinavian *groen* ('green') and *land* ('earth').

## GUÈRE

*Il n'y a guère lieu de s'inquiéter.*[12]

*Guère* cannot be used without *ne* (*ne…guère*) and the expression means 'not much', 'not really'.

10. We were contemplating magnificent Greek amphorae.
11. This explorer started an expedition in Greenland.
12. There is no cause for worry.

## H (Aspirated)

The '*h*' of Germanic, English or Oriental origin is aspirated. (See Haricot).

The following words and their derivatives have an aspirated '*h*':

| | | | | |
|---|---|---|---|---|
| *ha !* | *habanera* | *hâbler* | *Habsbourg* | *hache* |
| *hagard* | *haie* | *haîe* | *haillon* | *Hainaut* |
| *haine* | *haïr* | *haire* | *halage* | *halbran* |
| *hâle* | *haler* | *haleter* | *hall* | *halle* |
| *hallebarde* | *hallier* | *halo* | *haloir* | *halot* |
| *halotechnie* | *halte* | *halurgie* | *hamac* | *hameau* |
| *hampe* | *hamster* | *han* | *hanap* | *hanche* |
| *hand-ball* | *handicap* | *hangar* | *hanneton* | *Hanovre* |
| *hanse* | *hanter* | *happe* | *happelourde* | *happer* |
| *haquenée* | *haquet* | *hara-kiri* | *harangue* | *haras* |
| *harasser* | *harceler* | *harde* | *hardes* | *hardi* |
| *harem* | *hareng* | *hargneux* | *haricot* | *haridelle* |
| *harnais* | *haro* | *harpe* | *harper* | *harpie* |
| *harpon* | *hart* | *hasard* | *haschich* | *hase* |
| *haste* | *hâte* | *hâtelet* | *hâtier* | *hauban* |
| *haubert* | *hausse* | *haut* | *hautain* | *hautbois* |
| *Hautesse* | *havane* | *hâve* | *havir* | *havre* |
| *havresac* | *hayer* | *hé !* | *heaume* | *hein* |
| *héler* | *hem* | *henné* | *hennir* | *Henriade* |
| *héraut* | *hercher* | *hère* | *hérisser* | *hernie* |
| *héron* | *héros* | *herse* | *hêtre* | *heurt* |
| *hi !* | *hibou* | *hic* | *hideux* | *hie* |
| *hiérarchie* | *hile* | *hisser* | *ho !* | *hobereau* |
| *hoc* | *hoca* | *hocco* | *hoche* | *hocher* |
| *hockey* | *holà !* | *Hollande* | *hom !* | *homard* |
| *home* | *honchets* | *hongre* | *Hongrie* | *honnir* |
| *honte* | *hop !* | *hoquet* | *hoqueton* | *horde* |
| *horion* | *hors* | *hospodar* | *hotte* | *Hottentot* |
| *hou !* | *houblon* | *houe* | *houille* | *houle* |
| *houlette* | *houlque* | *houp !* | *houper* | *houppe* |

| | | | | |
|---|---|---|---|---|
| *houppelande* | *hourailler* | *hourd* | *houret* | *houri* |
| *hourque* | *hourra !* | *Hourvari* | *houseaux* | *houspiller* |
| *houssaie* | *housse* | *housser* | *houssine* | *houssoir* |
| *houx* | *hoyau* | *huard* | *hublot* | *huche* |
| *hucher* | *huchet* | *hue !* | *huer* | *huette* |
| *huguenot* | *huhau !* | *huis clos* | *huit* | *huitaine* |
| *hulotte* | *hululer* | *humer* | *Hun* | *hune* |
| *huppe* | *hure* | *hurler* | *Huron* | *hussard* |
| *hutin* | *hutte* | | | |

Elision before the '*h*–' [This complex issue is discussed in detail in Grevisse's *Le Bon Usage* §48b (1993 ed.)]:

A number of rules can help us to decide whether to elide or not:

(a) Germanic or English names, in their original form, generally have an aspirated *h* (i.e. without liaison): *Heidegger*, *Hanovre*, *Harlem*.

(b) Names which have become fully integrated into French, like *Henri*, *Hubert*, *Hugues*, *Hugo* can either be aspirated or not. There is liaison in *Saint Hubert*.

(c) For reasons of euphony, we find *de Hitler* rather than *d'Hitler*, but *qu'Hitler* more often than *que Hitler*. We speak of *l'hitlérisme*.

(d) We say *La Havane*.

Why do we say *le héros* but *l'héroïne*?

—Only the word *héros* has an aspirated '*h*' – none of the other related words does (*héroïne*, *héroïque*, *héroïnomane*). In *héros*, the aspirated '*h*' is often justified by the fact that it allows speakers to avoid an unwanted homophony: *les héros* with *les zéros*: however, an internet forum[1] gives the following explanation:

1. See http://fr.answers.yahoo.com/question/index?qid=20091112001459AApEzSc.

*« On entrevoit une explication dans le fait que le mot-souche héros est très ancien dans la langue (et donc formé directement sur le grec), alors que tous les autres mots sont apparus successivement et plus tardivement si bien qu'on n'a plus tenu compte de l'aspect aspiré du 'h' ».*[2]

Pronunciation of the aspirated '*h*' started to disappear at the end of the Middle Ages (Grevisse and Goosse: 1993, 79). However, the aspirated '*h*' (of Germanic origin) would have been pronounced up until the 15th or 16th century. In fact, according to Professor Alex Vanneste (Antwerp): 'We can sometimes still hear it in Normandy and in Lorraine. But otherwise it has disappeared and now only functions as a diacritic sign preventing elision – *la hache* (the ax) vs. *l'hôtel* (the hotel).' [—Vanneste (private communication), January 2014].

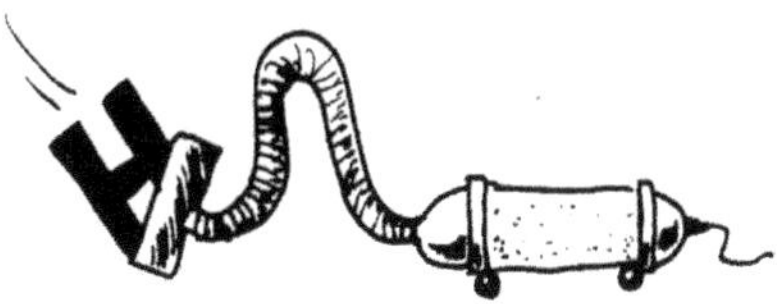

## HAÏR

*Me hait-il autant que nous le haïssons ?*[3]
*Elle hait les habitants de ce village.*

The verb *haïr* preserves the diaeresis on the *ï*, except in the three persons of the singular of the present indicative, and in the second person singular of the imperative.

It is the only verb that does not have a circumflex at the first and second person plural: *nous haïmes ; vous haïtes.*

## HAÏTI

*Nous sommes allés en Haïti cet été de 1988.*

The two constructions *aller en Haïti /aller à Haïti* are used but the former is generally considered more correct and is more common.

2. 'There is a possible explanation in the fact that the root word *héros* is very old in French (and was formed directly from Greek), whereas all the other words appeared successively and belatedly, and so the aspirated nature of the "*h*" was disregarded.'
3. Does he hate me as much as we hate him?

## HARICOT

*Je n'aime pas les haricots verts.*

The *'h'* of *haricot* is aspirated like most words beginning in *ha-*. Therefore we say *le haricot*, and there is no liaison in *les haricots verts*.

The *haricot* came originally from Mexico: the silent *h-* has subsequently been added to the written form.

See also: H (Aspirated)

## HAUT

*Il a mis la barre très haut.*

The adverb *haut* is used in this figurative expression to signify 'to put oneself at a high level' (closely corresponding with 'to set the bar very high' in English). The non-standard use of the adjective *haute* instead of the adverb is very frequent.

## HÉMISTICHE

*Voilà un bel hémistiche que nous offre le poète.*[4] Always masculine.

## HÉRAUT

*Keats est l'un des hérauts de la poésie romantique en Angleterre.*[5]

A homophone of the word *héros*, *héraut* means 'herald', 'bard', 'messenger'. As in *héros*, the *'h'* is aspirated.

Keats

## HÉROS

*Héros* comes from the ancient Greek: ἥρως, *hếrôs*.

See: H (Aspirated)

4. Here, the poet presents us with a beautiful hemistich (/half line of verse).

5. Keats is one of the heralds of Romantic poetry in England.

## HEURE

*À l'heure /À temps.*

*À l'heure* = 'at the arranged time' (8:30, 9:00, etc.)

*À temps* = 'in time,' i.e. before something starts.

*Sois là à temps* = 'Don't arrive late.'

This expression is also frequently used to indicate, after the event, that someone managed to make everything happen at the right time. Even though preparations started later than planned, the work was still finished at the desired time (World Fair, preparations for the Olympic Games, for example).

*Envoyez votre demande à temps* (i.e. before it is too late).

*Il a fini son exercice à temps* (at the time required).

## HEXAGONE

*Il a parcouru les quatre coins de l'Hexagone à la recherche des accents des Français avec son magnétophone.*[6]

The word *Hexagone* is capitalised when it denotes metropolitan France. If we look at the map of France from above, the territory seems to be a six-sided polygon, from which is derived the analogy to a hexagon.

## HIATUS

*L'hiatus en français est très fréquent.*

The *'h'* is not aspirated.

## HI-HAN

*Les hi-han de l'âne se faisaient de plus en plus fort alors qu'il avançait dans la montée du village.*[7]

Word of onomatopoeic origin, which is always invariable.

6. He travelled all over France with his tape recorder, in search of French accents.

7. The donkey brayed louder and louder as it travelled up the hill to the village.

## HORMIS

*Personne hormis ses fils ne lui était digne de confiance.*[8]

Adverb that always ends in '–*s*'. It derives from *hors* + *mis*.

In French, pronouns like *personne*, *chacun*, and *rien* are always singular, hence the singular verb form *était* in the example above.

## HUGUENOT

*Les huguenots étaient pendant les guerres de religion des protestants français.*[9]

The noun *huguenot* takes a lower-case initial letter, like *calviniste* and *catholique*.

## HUMEUR / HUMOUR

*Il est d'une humeur massacrante.*[10]
*Elle a un humour très mordant.*[11]

*Humeur* is feminine; *humour* masculine.

English humour is often indefinable and the French are often unable to appreciate it or even to understand it, as Patrice Leconte's 1996 film *Ridicule* showed. Note also that in the French section of the small bilingual pocket dictionary *Nugent* from 1784, there is no French entry *humour* and that in the English section, *humour* is translated by the French *humeur*. As Alain Rey's *Dictionnaire Historique* shows, the word *humour*, considered to be « *une spécialité bien anglaise* », and originally borrowed from English, comes itself from the Old French *humeur* (attested from 1725).

8. He did not trust anyone, except for his sons.
9. The Huguenots were members of the French protestant church during the Wars of Religion.
10. He is in a horrible mood.
11. She has a biting wit.

## HYMNE

*La Marseillaise est l'hymne national de la France.*[12]

Always masculine except when it denotes a liturgical song in Latin.

## HYPHEN

The appearance of the hyphen in France dates from the 16th century with the early days of printing. At first quite limited, its usage increased in the 17th century. Inspired by the Greek hyphen, it was originally used « *pour marquer l'union de deux lettres ou de deux parties d'un mot* » (Bailly, A., *Dictionnaire grec-français*, Paris: Hachette, 1901) and was later generalized to the use of compound nouns (*passe-temps*) or in cases where there was an inversion between the subject and verb (*promettez-vous*). It was initially represented as an upside-down omega: -ᴗ-, before appearing as a horizontal dash.[13]

One would write *une robe bleu clair* (without a hyphen when two adjectives are juxtaposed), but when an adjective of colour is modified by another, the two adjectives are invariable and they are separated with an hyphen: *cette cravate bleu-vert.* There is no hyphen when an adjective is followed by a noun: *une couverture vert pomme.*

See Double Hyphen.

12. The Marseillaise is France's national anthem.
13. For more details, see *Les mots à trait d'union* (Mathieu-Colas, Michel, Paris: Didier Erudition, 1994).

## I

Normally there is no liaison in the expression *mettre les points sur les i*, except for emphasis.

In Alfred de Musset's *Ballade à la lune* there must have been a liaison for *un i* to rhyme with *jauni* :

*C'était dans la nuit*
*Brune*
*Sur le clocher jauni*
*La lune*
*Comme un point sur un i.*

See also Œ.

MUSSET

## IBID. AND IBIDEM

*Ibid.* and *Ibidem*: the former is an abbreviation of the latter. Both are usually written in italics and there is normally a full stop after *Ibid.* (e.g. *Ibid.*, 43).

## IMPERATIVE

The second-person singular of the imperative of '*–er*' verbs takes an '*s*' before the pronouns *en* and *y* for euphony, in order to avoid the hiatus (*manges-en*, *penses-y*).

In Old French the imperative was sometimes constructed with an '*–s*' and sometimes without. In the Renaissance, grammarians stipulated that the form with an '*–s*' would be the indicative and the form without an '*–s*' would be the imperative. However, since the form before *en* and *y* in the imperative to avoid the hiatus was already in place, the '*–s*' here was maintained.

In the imperative, the hyphen is placed between the verb and the personal pronoun:

*parle-lui-en, donne-m'en, venons-en à l'essentiel.*

The imperative form of *aller* does not normally take an '*–s*' except when it is followed by a vowel sound: *va-t'en*, *vas-y*.

## IMPERFECT

*Un collègue argentin me disait aujourd'hui que le gouvernement devra faire preuve d'humilité.*[1]

In the following case, *disait* is simply a narrative use of the imperfect. Compared to the use of a passé composé, it is mainly a style effect. The fact is considered from the inside, in its unfolding, in the manner of a freeze-frame.

## IMPERFECT / PAST HISTORIC

Example 1:

(a) *Le ciel se couvrait de nuages.*

(b) *Le ciel se couvrit de nuages.*

With the use of the imperfect as in (a) above, the action is progressive. We can see the action happening (as in the construction *le ciel était en train de se couvrir de nuages*).

In (b), which uses the past historic, the action had happened and was complete at that moment in the past.

Example 2:

(a) *C'était en 1987 qu'il se rendait en France.*

(b) *C'était en 1987 qu'il se rendit en France.*

Sentence (a) answers the question 'when was he in France?' and is descriptive. We cast our minds back to the time when he was there.

Sentence (b) on the other hand describes a punctual fact, with no emphasis on duration but rather on the fact that the action was completed by this date.

## IMPERFECT SUBJUNCTIVE

The imperfect subjunctive belongs to the literary register. In written language, the third person singular is most often used. With the exception of the auxiliaries, the other forms of the verb have fallen out of use.

1. An Argentine colleague told me today that the government will have to show humility.

Example 1:

*Elle poursuivit sa diatribe, les yeux vides, le visage grimaçant et enlaidi, sa colère la propulsant vers Jean jusqu'à ce qu'elle lui hurlât en pleine figure.*[2]

*Elle poursuivit sa diatribe, les yeux vides, le visage grimaçant et enlaidi, sa colère la propulsant vers Jean jusqu'au moment où elle lui hurla en pleine figure.*[3]

– Imperfect subjunctive: hypothetical consequence.

– Past historic: real consequence.

*Elle poursuivit sa diatribe, les yeux vides, le visage grimaçant et enlaidi, sa colère la propulsant vers Jean au point qu'elle lui hurlait en pleine figure.*

– Imperfect: the speaker is emphasising the duration of the action.

Example 2:

*Il entra dans la salle la main tendue comme pour saisir la poignée de la porte d'un wagon avant que le train, déjà en marche, ne prît de la vitesse et quittât le quai.*[4]

*Il entra dans la salle la main tendue comme pour saisir la poignée de la porte d'un wagon avant que le train, déjà en marche, ne prenne de la vitesse et quitte le quai.*

– Opinion is divided over the lack of tense concord, and the use of the present rather than the imperfect subjunctive. The imperfect subjunctive adds a very literary – indeed archaic – connotation to the sentence. A writer today can choose not to use the imperfect subjunctive in a more informal style.

Example 3:

*Je rêvais d'une femme qui* ***fût*** *belle.*

'I was dreaming of a woman and I wanted her to be beautiful.'

2. She continued her tirade, her eyes expressionless, her face grotesquely contorted, her anger propelling her towards Jean until she shouted at him, full in the face.

3. She continued her tirade, her eyes expressionless, her face grotesquely contorted, her anger propelling her towards Jean until the moment when she shouted at him, full in the face.

4. He entered the room, his hand stretched out as if to grab the carriage door handle before the train, which was already moving, sped up and left the platform.

*Je rêvais d'une femme qui **fut** belle.*
'I was dreaming of a women who was once beautiful.'

EXAMPLE 4:

*Il fallut /faudrait que vous lussiez ?*

– *Il fallut que vous lussiez* (it was necessary that you should read) is the simple application of the classic rule of the agreement of tenses (used mainly in literature).

– *Il faudrait que vous lussiez* (it would be necessary that you read) is a special case. It is employing the imperfect of the subjunctive after a conditional that maintains its present tense value.

In the past, one would have written *il aurait fallu* (it would have been necessary) or *il eût fallu que vous lussiez* (it should have been necessary that you read).

N.B.: The correction of French spelling in 1990 that abolished the circumflex accent on the *'i'* and the *'e'* does not apply to the preceding case where the distinction must be made between the indicative and the subjunctive.

## IMPERFECT SUBJUNCTIVE (HYPERCORRECT USAGE)

In French the present subjunctive replaces the imperfect which is now hardly used (except in literary narration). Nicolas Sarkozy's sentence, used after the departure of his minister Jean-Louis Borloo, « *j'aurais d'ailleurs préféré qu'il restât* » (Tuesday 16 November 2010 – Palais de l'Elysée) was disparaged by the media. It came across as anachronistic in spoken language, and more appropriate for a written register. It is an indicator of hypercorrection.

SARKOZY & BORLOO

## IMPOSSIBLE

*C'est impossible que nous oubliions notre rendez-vous.*

The expression *il /c'est impossible que* requires the subjunctive.

## INCARNAT

Colour adjective ('crimson') derived from a noun, but one which is an exception to the rule and therefore agrees normally: *des ongles incarnats.*

See AMARANTE, ÉCARLATE, FAUVE, MAUVE, POURPRE, and ROSE.

## INCONGRU

*Nous avons fait une rencontre incongrue la nuit dernière.*

Without a diaeresis in the feminine.

## INDE / INDES

*Nous avons voyagé en Inde /aux Indes.*

When India was not a single country, it was known by the plural name *les Indes*. Today, we talk only of *l'Inde* (singular without the '-*s*'), except when referring to historical subjects, as, for example, in the expression *les Indes Occidentales* ('the West Indies').

## INDENTATION

It is difficult to determine the exact origin of the indent /indentation. The word appeared for the first time in the French language in the *Correspondance* of Jean-Louis Guez de Balzac (1654) where he pointed out « *la séparation par renforcement du début du texte, d'un début de paragraphe* » ('the separation by reinforcement of the beginning of the text, of the beginning of the paragraph') —Rey: 1998, p. 84.

« *A vostre loisir, écrit-il à son correspondant, vous me ferez copier ... la Harangue de La Casa parce que je désire la mettre dans une préface à la fin des Lettres choisies. Mais je voudrais que la copie fust [divisée] en plusieurs sections, ou (pour parler comme Rocollet) en des a linea, comme sont tous mes discours, qui est une chose qui aide extrêmement celui qui lit et démesle bien la confusion des espèces* ».

'At your leisure,' he writes to his correspondent, 'you will copy for me...the *Harangue of La Casa* because I wish to put it in a preface at the end of Selected Letters. But I request that the copy be [divided] into several sections, or (to speak like Rocollet) into several "*a lineas*", as are all my discourses, which is something that is extremely helpful to the one who reads and untangles the confusion of the elements [of the text].'

Guez de Balzac

## INDICATIVE / SUBJUNCTIVE

Example 1:

*Il n'y a rien qui soit impossible.*

The subjunctive is often used when a relative pronoun is found after a negative expression or in an interrogative or conditional sentence. The indicative can be used when talking about a collective subject that can be perceived:

*Parmi les articles que vous me présentez, il n'y a rien qui me plaît.*

We can also write:

*il n'y a rien qui me plaise* (i.e. which could possibly please me).

The conditional is also found:

*Il n'est personne ici qui ne voudrait quitter le pays.*

Example 2:

(a) *Elle imagine qu'il a fait du cheval.*

(b) *Elle imagine qu'il ait fait du cheval.*

In (a), in her mind she sees him as someone who has gone horse riding, or she genuinely believes that he has gone horse riding.

In (b), in her mind she sees him as someone who might have gone horse riding, even though she knows that he has not.

Example 3:

*Il est certain qu'il viendra.*

*Il n'est pas rare qu'il soit malade.*

The indicative is used after an impersonal verb in the following situations:

(i) if the main verb is affirmative;

(ii) and if there is virtual certainty.

Example 4:
*Je n'ai jamais eu de bijoux qui vaillent deux sous.*[5]

The present subjunctive is used here because it is an estimate rather than an established value.

Example 5:
What is the difference between

*c'est le plus joli chien que j'ai jamais eu /j'aie jamais eu* –?

—In the indicative, the sentence is an affirmation: 'I have had several dogs and that one is the nicest.' The subjunctive, on the other hand, brings with it the idea of possibility, opportunity, and chance: 'That is the nicest dog that I have had the opportunity to own.'

Example 6:
*Est-il vrai qu'il est allé /soit allé chez ses parents* –?

– The use of the indicative (*est allé*) implies that the speaker believes the person has gone and visited his parents. The question is almost meant to check a piece of information that the speaker believes to be true.

– The subjunctive (*soit allé*) implies that the speaker questions the person's visit to his parents. The latter is presented as unreal.

## INFINITIVE CONSTRUCTIONS

*On entend tomber la pluie /On entend la pluie tomber.*[6]

The first formulation is the most common. In the first case, the simple fact that rain is falling – that it is raining – is noted. In the second case, the word *pluie* is slightly emphasized, as it immediately follows the verb.

## INTERPELLER

*Le dictateur a été interpellé pour crime contre l'humanité.*[7]

This verb is always spelled with a double *'l'*, unlike *appeler* which only takes a double *'l'* before *–e*, *–es*, *–ent*.

*Interpeller* comes from classical Latin (*interpellare*) and from legal Latin, while *appeler* comes from classical Latin

5. I never had any jewelry worth more than a penny
6. One hears the rain falling /One hears the falling rain.
7. The dictator was questioned for crimes against humanity.

*appellare* (used to mean 'call' in Vulgar Latin, in place of the more formal *vocare*).

## INVERSION OF SUBJECT AND VERB

In a literary register, inversion is common: *aimé-je*, *chanté-je*, etc.

*Aimé-je le français plus que toute autre langue ?*

The acute accent pronounced as a grave is mandatory for an acceptable pronunciation (otherwise it would be pronounced /aimje/, as the 'e' is silent).

Inversion is common in the following situations:

(a) after *tel : Être ou ne pas être, telle est la question.*

(b) in some hypothetical or optative set expressions: *Plût à Dieu* ; *Vive la France* ; *L'aurait-il su* ; *cela ne serait jamais arrivé.*

(c) after a relative pronoun for stylistic effect: *Il observait dans le ciel les nuages que poussait la bise.*

(d) to create emphasis or a literary effect: *Se fit alors entendre le hurlement d'un loup.*

(e) in a legal register: *Sera poursuivie toute personne ayant pénétré en ces lieux sans autorisation.*

## ISRAËL

*Les pourparlers entre Israël et les États-Unis pourraient reprendre en juin.*[8]

*Israël* should be used without an article. Although the pronunciation in /s/ is the one prescribed by dictionaries, the pronunciation in /z/ is also heard.

See also NAMES OF COUNTRIES.

## ISSU

*Elle était issue d'une famille bourgeoise.*

Past participle of the defective verb *issir.*

The present participle *issant(e)* is used in heraldry:

*Sur l'écu se trouvaient des licornes issantes d'une rivière.*[9]

8. Talks between Israel and the United States could resume in June.

9. On the shield were unicorns issuing from a river.

## JADIS

*Jadis on lisait davantage.*

The final '*–s*' of *jadis* is pronounced.

## JAMAIS

*C'est la plus belle histoire que j'aie jamais lue.*

What is the origin of this *jamais* in French which does not have negative force?

—*Jamais* is positive: *umquam* in classical Latin, which meant 'one day', 'at a certain time' (in English, 'ever').

*Ne … jamais* is negative: *numquam* (*ne umquam*) in classical Latin, which meant 'never', 'not a single day', 'not a single time'.

## JEÛNER

*Jeûner* ('to fast'), like *jeûne*, takes a circumflex, but *à jeun* ('fasting') does not.

*Déjeuner* means literally 'to break the fast.'

GANDHI

## JOUR (SE FAIRE)

*De nouvelles idées se sont fait jour et il les a couchées sur le papier.*[1]

The past participle *fait* is always invariable in the expression *se faire jour*.

## JOUR DE LA SEMAINE

*La semaine des quatre jeudis.*

The names of days of the week, just like the names of the months, are common nouns. They are therefore variable in number (i.e. can be pluralised), and are written with lower case initial letters.

1. New ideas came to life and he put them down on paper.

## JOVIAL

*Les employés de cette entreprise sont pour la plupart joviaux et sympathiques.*[2]

*Jovial* like *astral, austral, boréal, brutal, glacial, idéal, natal, pascal* forms its plural by adding '*-aux*'.

*Banal, bancal, fatal, final, naval* form their plurals by adding an '*-s*'.

## JURER (SE)

*Ils se sont juré de se taire.*

Invariable: '*se*' is indirect.

## KAKI

As a colour adjective, *kaki* is invariable: *des pantalons kaki.*

The word has been borrowed into French from English, but is originally from Urdu (*khākī* : 'dusty') and Hindi (—Rey: 1998, 1944): its invariability stems from this fact.

2. Generally speaking, this company's employees are cheerful and kind.

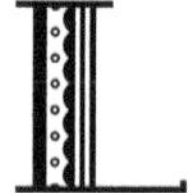

## LABEUR

*C'est un dur labeur que d'éplucher des pommes de terre.*[1]

The word *labeur* is masculine. *Labor* was masculine in Latin.

## LAÏC / LAÏQUE

*L'école laïque est une chose bien française.*[2]

*Ces chrétiens que l'on appelle laïcs !*[3]

*Laïque* is the feminine form of *laïc.*

In the masculine, both forms are found, but rarely: *un enseignement laic / laïque.*

## LAISSER (IMPERATIVE)

*Laisse-le faire.*

The only situation in which *lui* can be used with *laisser* is when the word functions as the indirect object, as in the following example:

*Ne joue pas avec l'ours en peluche de ta sœur : laisse-le lui !*[4]

In the following sentence, lui is the indirect object of the verb *faire* and not *laisser :*

*Qu'on ne le laisse pas lui faire du tort.*

(i.e. *Qu'on ne laisse pas cette personne lui faire du tort*).[5]

1. Peeling potatoes is hard work.
2. Secular schools are a very French concept.
3. These so-called secular Christians!
4. Don't play with your sister's teddy bear – leave it to her!
5. May he be guarded from doing harm.

## LAISSER + INFINITIVE

*Les feuilles de papier que j'ai laissé/laissées tomber.*[6]

Some grammarians and authors (Grevisse and Goosse: 1993, 1342), taking the view that *laissé* and the following infinitive form a periphrasis analogous to *fait* + infinitive, do not recommend agreement. *Littré* does not disagree, although it notes that agreement prevails in practice today. *Les feuilles de papier que j'ai laissé tomber* is more common.

If agreement is applied, the feminine plural in the example above is *laissées*, because it is the leaves (*feuilles*, feminine plural) which are falling (i.e. *tu as laissé les feuilles tomber*).

Compare:

*Elle s'est laissée mourir ; elle s'est laissée aller ;*

and

*Elle s'est laissé vaincre.*[7]

## LAMBDA

*Les étudiants de cette école ne sont pas des étudiants lambda.*[8]

This invariable adjective is the name of the Greek letter (λ) in opposition to alpha (α).

## LAS

*Je suis las de toute cette affaire.*

The final 's' of *las* ('weary') is not pronounced, unlike the feminine *lasse.*

## LAURIER

In the plural:

*des lauriers-cerises,*
*des lauriers-roses,*
but *des lauriers-sauce* ('bay-trees' /'bay-leaves').

6. The sheets of paper that I dropped.
7. She let her opponent win.
8. The students of this school are not *lambda* (average /'B-stream') students.

## LE (Impersonal Pronoun)

*On ne naît pas femme, on le devient.*[9]

Why do we not say *on la devient* here? Here *femme* is being used as an adjective rather than a noun. We would write: *On ne naît pas intelligent, on le devient. Femme* is a subject attribute and therefore not a direct object. A subject attribute is always pronominalised in the masculine (*elle semble jolie à mes yeux – elle le semble à mes yeux*).

## LE / LA PLUS

*La Provence est la région que j'ai /j'aie le plus aimée.*[10]

'Provence is the region that I have loved most' (i.e. to the highest degree): this is a response to the question: *Quelle est la région que vous avez aimée le plus ?*

Before an adjective in the relative superlative (superlative with *le plus, le moins...*), the article is invariable when the thing in question is compared only with itself (i.e. when the superlative can be replaced by 'to the highest degree'). We would therefore say: *C'est dans la journée que cette pierre est le plus lumineuse.*[11]

The article varies if comparison is being made between two (or more) different things: *Cette pierre est la plus précieuse de toutes.*[12]

## LEDIT / LADITE

*Je suis absolument contre ledit traité.*[13]
*Ladite loi fut rejetée en 1920.*[14]

Written as a single word.

9. One is not born, but becomes, a woman.
10. Provence is the region that I liked the most.
11. This stone is at its brightest during the day.
12. This stone is the most precious of all.
13. I am completely against the aforementioned treaty.
14. The aforementioned law was rejected in 1920.

## LEITMOTIV

*La musique de Bizet est l'un des leitmotive /leitmotivs du film.*[15]

The plural is either *leitmotive* or *leitmotivs*, corresponding to the form of the plural in the source language, German (—Rey: 1998, 2297).

## LEQUEL / LAQUELLE

*La façon avec laquelle tu parles est maladroite.*[16]

This expression is frequently cited on the Internet in very serious texts. However, it is either a literal translation from the English or a malapropism, and therefore the use of *dont* is preferable (or simply « *ta façon de parler…* »).

*La femme de laquelle /dont /de qui je parle…*

'The woman of which /of whom I speak…'

*Dont* (of whom):

The most frequently employed pronoun, no matter what the antecedent.

= 'I speak of a woman and what I am going to say relates to her.'

*De laquelle* (of whom):

= 'There are several women, and I am speaking about one of them. What I am going to say relates to her.'

*De qui* (of whom, informal):

= 'The woman is the person of whom I speak.'

*De qui* is used only if the antecedent is a person.

## LIAISON

Liaisons are normally divided into three categories:

invariable,
variable, and
hypercorrect liaisons:

The table on the following page, based on a Chart of Liaisons from Encrevé, [*La liaison avec et sans enchaînement…* (1988), 47 ; also in Lodge *et al*, (1997), 99], schematizes the different types of liaison. –

15. Bizet's music is one of the leitmotifs of the film.
16. The way in which you speak is awkward.

| | Invariable | Variable | Hypercorrect |
|---|---|---|---|
| Noun phrase | Determiner + noun or pronoun or adjective | Plural noun + adjective, or verb | Singular noun + adjective, or verb |
| | *vos_enfants*<br>*deux_autres*<br>*vos_anciens amis* | *des soldats_anglais*<br>*ses plans_ont réussi* | *un soldat_anglais*<br>*son plan_a réussi* |
| Verb group | Pronoun + verb | Verb + complement | |
| | *ils_ont compris*<br>*nous en_avons* | *je vais_essayer*<br>*j'avais_entendu*<br>*vous êtes_invité* | |
| | Verb + pronoun | *il commençait_a lire*<br>*c'est_un village* | |
| | *allons_y*<br>*ont_ils compris* | *il est_impossible*<br>*on est_obligé* | |
| Uninflected words | | Invariable monosyllabic words | *Et* + whatever follows |
| | | *en_une journée*<br>*très_interessant* | *et_on l'a fait* |
| | | Invariable polysyllabic words | |
| | | *pendant_un jour*<br>*toujours_utile* | |
| Special cases | Set phrases | | Aspirated *'h'*<br>*des_héros*<br>*en_haut* |
| | *comment_allez-vous?*<br>*les États_Unis*<br>*de temps_en temps*<br>*tout_à coup* | | Article etc. + relevant numerals<br>*cent_huitième*<br>*en_onze jours*<br>*le un* (no liaison) |

Encrevé makes a distinction between invariable and variable liaisons to avoid any prescriptivist terms such as 'compulsory', 'optional' and 'forbidden.'

*Les pays autant latins que nordiques valent la peine un jour ou l'autre d'être visités.*[17]

In this example, there is no grammatical connection between *pays* and *autant* (compare *les pays ennemis* in which there is a grammatical connection). There can even be a pause here (*les pays – autant latins que nordiques…*).

For these two reasons there is no liaison.

In his analysis of political discourse, Encrevé (1988: 183) distinguishes another form of linking in other words: *La liaison sans enchaînement* ('liaison without linking'). *Enchaînement* signifies the pronunciation of the final consonant of one word at the onset of the following syllable, as if it was the first letter of the following word. There is also a pause between the two words: « *Il faut interdire* » is pronounced literally « *Il fau* [PAUSE] *t-interdire* ».

See also TOUJOURS.

## LIEUE

*Il était à cent lieues de s'imaginer qu'elle était sa fille.*[18]

*Une lieue* is a measurement of distance (English 'league'), of around four to seven kilometres (which length varied from time to time and from country to country). Not to be confused with *un lieu* ('pollack', a type of fish).

20 000 LIEUES SOUS LES MERS

17. Latin countries and Nordic countries are equally worth a visit some day.
18. He had absolutely no idea that she was his daughter.

## LONGTEMPS

*Longtemps j'ai pensé à ce que vous m'aviez dit.*

This phrase has a literary style without being archaic. The positioning of the adverb of time 'often' – placed in first position (instead of being placed between the auxiliary and the past participle) – serves only to mark an insistence on the duration. Furthermore, this positioning marks a rupture in the rhythm of the sentence, as if to denounce an imbalance due to the abnormal length of the reflection. Rhythmically, it is more melodious to say: *J'ai longtemps pensé à ce que vous m'aviez dit.*

## LORSQUE / QUAND

*Lorsqu'elle / Quand elle reviendra je lui en parlerai.*

The difference between *lorsque* and *quand* is purely stylistic, the former being more literary.

In indirect or direct questions, however, as a subordinating conjunction rather than an adverb, *lorsque* cannot be used:

*Je me demandais quand elle reviendrait* (but *Je lui poserai la question, lorsqu'elle reviendra*) ;

*Quand viendra-t-il ?*

## LYCÉE

*Ce lycée est l'un des meilleurs que je connaisse.*

This word ends in *-ée* and, like *gynécée*, *musée*, and *empyrée*, is masculine.

## MALGRÉ QUE

Only the expression *malgré que j'en aie* ('however reluctantly') is accepted by purists. All other usages of *malgré que* + verb are considered to be non-standard and belong to the spoken register.

*Malgré le fait que* followed with either the indicative (one insists on the reality of a fact) or the subjunctive (this remains a supposition) is absolutely acceptable: *Il est resté en bons termes avec lui malgré le fait qu'il l'a /l'ait insulté.*[1]

## MARAIS / MARÉE

*Le marais poitevin est aussi appelé la Venise verte.*[2]
*Il faut toujours se méfier de la marée, lorsque l'on va à la pêche au couteaux.*[3]

*Le marais* translates as a marsh or swamp and should not be confused with *la marée* ('the tide'). Le Marais is a fashionable district in the 3rd and 4th arrondissement of Paris, which is famous for its numerous art galleries.

## MARCHER

*Les kilomètres qu'il a marchés ; les 100 miles qu'il a marché.* See VIVRE.

## MARRON

As a colour adjective, *marron* is invariable: *des meubles marron.*

With the sense of 'crooked /corrupt', it agrees in gender and number: *un médecin marron*; *des esclaves marrons, des femmes marronnes.* This sense of the word comes from the Spanish *cimarrón* which means 'runaway', a word used to denote the slaves who escaped to regain their freedom.

1. He remained on good terms with him, despite the fact that he had insulted him.
2. The Marais Poitevin is also called 'Green Venice.'
3. You must always be wary of the tide when fishing for razor clams.

## MARTYR / MARTYRE

A *martyr* is a person who has suffered.

*Les martyrs de la Première Guerre mondiale.*

*Martyre* is torture, pain endured.

*Il a souffert le martyre.*

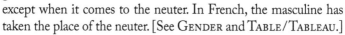

## MASCULINE / FEMININE

In general, the French word has the gender that the word had in Latin, except when it comes to the neuter. In French, the masculine has taken the place of the neuter. [See GENDER and TABLE/TABLEAU.]

In 1676, Father Bouhours, who strived for the masculine gender to take precedence over the feminine in agreement (e.g. *Pierre et Virginie sont allés au marché*) would have justified this rule by specifying that when the two genders meet, « *il faut que le plus noble l'emporte* »[4] (Bouhours: reprinted 1971, 120).

Agreement of gender between the adjective and the closest noun can be traced back to antiquity. This rule of proximity was commonly used in the 16th century. Some try to reintroduce it (*cf* the movement « *Que les hommes et les femmes soient belles* »)[5]

The following nouns ending in *-ée* are masculine:

*androcée, apogée, athénée, caducée, camée, colisée, conopée, coryphée, écomusée, empyrée, gynécée, hyménée, hypogée, lépidostée, lépisostée, lycée, macchabée, mausolée, musée, nymphée, périgée, périnée, pongée, propylée, protée, prytanée, pygmée, scarabée, sigisbée, spondée, trochée, trophée, zée.*

## M'AS-TU-VU

*Ce qu'elle est m'as-tu-vu !*[6]

This expression is invariable both as a noun and as an adjective (in the sense of 'pretentious').

4. 'The more noble triumphs' [1676 comment —Ed.].
5. See http://www.petitions24.net/regleproximite
6. She is such a show-off!

## MAUVE

Colour adjective which derives from a noun, but one of the exceptions which agrees normally: *des robes mauves.*

See Amarante, Écarlate, Fauve, Incarnat, Pourpre, and Rose.

## MAXIMAL / MAXIMUM

*L'avion se trouvait à son altitude maximale.*[7]

In common usage, maximum can be used as a noun or an adjective. The word maximal is exclusively an adjective, and there is a tendency to prefer it in formal language.

There is no difference of meaning between *maximum* and *maximal.*

## MÊME

Expressions with *même* :

(a) *même si :* 'but this should or could normally have been prevented by the fact that…' –
*Il est sorti de sa maison même s'il n'avait pas entendu l'alarme.*
*Il a persisté même s'il avait essuyé de nombreux échecs.*[8]
*Nous ne voulions pas aller au cinéma même s'il pleuvait.*

(b) *à même :* 'in direct physical contact with' –
*Il dormait à même le sol.*

(c) *à même de :* 'capable of' –
*Elle n'a pas été à même de parler, paralysée qu'elle était par la peur.*[9]

(d) *de même que :* 'in the same way that' –
*De même que la glace fond au soleil, le sucre fond à la chaleur.*[10]

(e) *lors même que /quand (bien) même*, or (more informally) *quand (bien) même que :* 'even if' /'even though' –
*Quand (bien) même il ferait soleil, nous resterions à l'intérieur bien au chaud.*[11]

7. The aircraft was at its maximum altitude.
8. Despite tasting defeat on multiple occasions, he persevered.
9. She was so paralysed by fear, that she could not utter a word.
10. Just as the sun melts ice-cream, heat melts sugar.
11. Even if it was sunny, we would stay inside, nice and warm.

(f) *par cela même que :* 'for the particular reason that' –
*Il est très doué en langues par cela même qu'il est capable de reconnaître l'allemand du hollandais.*[12]

(g) *quand même* or *tout de même :* 'the contrary normally having turned out to be the case' –
*Le joueur a perdu quand même.*

(h) *quand (bien) même que,* [regional: *quand même* (without '*que*')] –
*Quand même qu'il pleuvrait, je sortirais.*

(i) *tout de même que :* 'in exactly the same way that' / 'just as' –
*Tout de même que la glace fond au soleil, le sucre fond à la chaleur.*

(j) *de même :* 'the same' / 'in the same way' –
*Il s'éloigna et elle fit de même.*

(k) *sans même :* 'without' (emphatic) –
*Il écrivait sans même réfléchir.*

(l) *tout de même :* 'still' / 'all the same' –
*Quoi qu'elle lui dise, il divorcerait tout de même,* [or, *quand même : cf.* (g) *infra*].

## MESSEOIR

*Il messied de parler lorsque s'exprime le chef de la tribu.*[13]

Archaic verb meaning 'to be unbecoming to …'

## METTRE (SE)

*Elle s'est mise à rire de joie.*

This purely pronominal verb always takes the pronoun '*se*', and agrees with the subject.

## MIDI

*On se retrouve sur le midi.*

In spoken French, one would say *sur les midi* (invariable).

12. He has a gift for languages, which enables him to distinguish German from Dutch.
13. It is unseemly to talk when the tribe chief is speaking.

## MIE

*Je ne mange mie* (= *'une miette'*).

The expression *ne...mie* is very archaic and literary in register. In Old French, particles expressing small quantity reinforced the negation: *ne...goutte*, *ne...mie* (which comes from *mie*, the doughy part of bread which is not the crust), and *ne...point* (which is still in standard use today).

## MILLE

*Il fallait parcourir cinq mille kilomètres avant de rejoindre la terre ferme.*[14]

*Mille* is invariable. In a date it can be written *mille*, or more rarely *mil*, when it is followed by one or several numbers [*mil(le) neuf cent quatre-vingt-dix* but *l'an deux mille*].

*Mille* derives from the Latin *milia /millia*, plural of L. *mille* (*'milie'*, early 12th century, in *Voyage de Charlemange*) with variant *mil* from Latin *mille*.[15]

[*Mille* (meaning 'mile' – from L. *mille passuum*) may vary.]

See also CENT and VINGT.

## MIS À PART

*Mis à part quelques fautes de genre, il parlait plutôt bien le français.*[16]
*Quelques fautes de genre mises à part, il parlait plutôt bien le français.*[17]

Invariable when placed before the noun; variable when it follows. It is invariable when it can be substituted by a preposition (e.g. *sauf*): *Sauf quelques fautes de genre, il parlait plutôt bien le français*. In the second sentence, it can be replaced by *exceptées* but not by *sauf*: *Quelques fautes de genre exceptées, il parlait plutôt bien le français.*

14. The nearest land was five thousand kilometres away.

15. —*Nouveau dictionnaire étymologique et historique*, Albert Dauzat, Jean Dubois, and Henri Mitterand (Paris: Larousse, 1964).

16. Aside from sometimes using the wrong gender, he spoke French rather well.

17. Some errors concerning gender aside, he spoke French rather well.

## MITTERRAND

MITTERRAND

*François Mitterrand fut Président de la République de 1981 à 1995.*

Spelled with a double 'r' and no accent because of the double consonant.

Not to be confused with Henri Mitterand, with a single 'r', best known as an author (with Albert Dauzat and Jean Dubois) of the *Nouveau dictionnaire étymologique et historique* (1964).

## MOEURS

*Les mœurs alimentaires ont bien évolué récemment.*

Good practice usually recommends not to pronounce the 's' of *mœurs* (morals), but as dictionaries attest, the pronunciation of the 's' is standard.

## MOINS (AU) / DU MOINS

*Il y a au moins quinze personnes dans la salle.*
*Je ne pense pas du moins qu'il ait raison.*

*Au moins* means 'at least', while *du moins* signifies 'at any rate'.

## MOMENT

*Au moment où il annonça l'arrivée de son père /Au moment qu'il annonça l'arrivée de son père, elle sortit précipitamment de la pièce.*[18]

*Au moment que* is an archaic and emphasized form of *au moment où*. These two structures are followed by the indicative.

## MONTRÉAL

*Montréal est une ville très cosmopolite.*

The 't' is not pronounced.

18. At the moment when he announced the arrival of his (or her) father, she quickly exited the room.

## MORAL / MORALE

*Le moral* denotes a mental or emotional condition.

*Manger du chocolat c'est bon pour le moral.*

*La morale* is the set of rules in an ethical code or a lesson that you learn from something:

*Les Fables de La Fontaine se terminent toujours par une morale.*[19]

## MOULT

*Il y a moult raisons de le croire.*[20] Invariable.

From the Latin *multum* (= *beaucoup*, *très*). Documentary evidence is inconclusive over whether the term was variable or invariable up until the 13th century, after which time it was considered an adverb. It disappeared from common usage in the 16th century, to be replaced by *beaucoup*, and has only subsequently been used in an elaborated register.

## MOURIR

Why do we say *il est mort* rather than *il est mouru*?

—In Latin, *mourir* was a deponent verb, that is, a verb with an active sense but taking passive form. The past participle in Latin was *mortuus*.

*Il est mort* corresponds to '*mortuus est*'.

*Il est né* corresponds to '*natus est*'.

## MOYEN ÂGE

*Le Moyen Âge est une période riche en superstitions.*

There are various possible spellings, with or without a hyphen, with or without a capital, but the normal written form is *le Moyen Âge*.

The adjective is *moyenâgeux*.

19. La Fontaine's Fables always conclude with a moral lesson.
20. There are ample reasons to believe it /him.

## MUSICAL NOTES

*J'en ai joué des sol et des do.* Always invariable.

The designation of musical notes *ut*, *ré*, *mi*, *fa*, *sol*, and *la* was given by the Tuscan monk Guido d'Arezzo (995–1050), by taking the first syllable of the first seven verses of *the Hymn of St John the Baptist* written in the 9th century by the poet Paul Diacre (circa 720 – circa 787):

***Ut*** *queant laxis*
***Re****sonare fibris*
***Mi****ra gestorum*
***Fa****muli tuorum*
***Sol****ve polluti*
***La****bii reatum*
*Sancte* ***I****ohannes*

The musical note *'si'*, originating from the last verse *Sancte Iohannes*, arrived later in the 16th century.

## NAMES OF COUNTRIES

In French, feminine names form the largest category of names of countries.

Masculine country names sometimes owe their gender to the fact that they originate as names of people. Before it was a State, 'Israel' was the name given to Jacob (a person of masculine gender) by God. Many names of African countries are masculine, because they are named after a river that was itself of masculine gender (*le Congo*, *le Sénégal*).

We remark that the tendency is to masculinize countries. The younger the country, the higher the likelihood that it is masculine: *l'Angola, le Nigeria*[1] (which became masculine in the 1970s), *le Botswana*, *le Canada*, *le Liberia*, or *le Vénézuela*.

*L'Iran*, *l'Iraq*, *Israël* (which has no article, as in English, because at the beginning it was a British mandate), and *l'Uruguay* are all masculine, whereas *l'Argentine*, *Cuba*, *l'Égypte*, *l'Inde*, *l'Irlande*, and *Madagascar* are feminine.

## NE (EXPLETIVE)

*J'ai peur qu'il ne vienne.*

The expletive *ne* belongs to a formal register. It indicates that the speaker is moving into a section which is hypothetical, rather than negative. Compare:

*Je crains qu'il ne vienne = J'ai peur, il viendra.*

*Je crains qu'il ne vienne pas = J'ai peur, il ne viendra pas.*

The expletive *ne* is used:

(a) After certain conjunctions: *avant que, à moins que.*

*Je ne viendrai pas à moins qu'il n'insiste.*

(b) After expressions of fear or prevention:

*J'ai peur qu'il ne lui en parle.*

*Pour éviter qu'il n'oublie ses verbes irréguliers, fais-les-lui réviser.*[2]

1. Also spelled *le Nigéria* and *le Libéria.*
2. So that he doesn't forget his irregular verbs, make him revise them.

(c) After an unequal comparison (*plus, moins, autre*):
*Vous parlez plus que vous n'agissez.*
*Elle est moins intelligente qu'on ne pourrait le penser.*
(d) After verbs of doubt and negation:
*Je doute qu'il ne prenne cet exercice au sérieux.*

## NE (Negation)

*Il ne pense jamais à son frère.*
*Personne n'est venu le rencontrer.*

In the expressions *ne jamais /jamais ne* and *ne personne /personne ne*, the particle *ne* is the real negation, and the other word was originally an adverb. *Personne* was an indefinite pronoun, like *rien*. Without *ne*, the sentence is colloquial.

*Penses-tu qu'elle ne se soit jamais demandé pourquoi personne ne l'aimait ?*[3]

In this example, the omission of the first *ne* does not downgrade the register (*Penses-tu qu'elle se soit jamais demandé pourquoi personne ne l'aimait ?)*, but the meaning changes from *Do you really think she never wondered why nobody liked her?* to *Do you think she ever wondered why nobody liked her?*.

## NE (Literary)

*Il ne cesse de parler en argot.*

By '*ne littéraire*' one refers to certain verbs and constructions in formal French that are used with *ne* but without *pas* in order to be negative. The use of *pas* in these constructions is merely optional.

The *ne littéraire* is used with seven verbs:

(1) *Cesser*, (2) *oser*, and (3) *pouvoir* do not need *pas* :
*Il n'ose (pas) s'exprimer en classe.*
(4) *Bouger*, (5) *daigner*, and (6) *manquer* are commonly used with *pas*, but could be used without:
*Elles ne daignent répondre à mes questions.*
(7) *Savoir* is a special case, as it can be used without *pas* when:
– it means *to be uncertain*:
*Je ne sais si c'est vrai ;*

3. Do you believe that she never wondered why no one loved her?

– it is used in the conditional:
*Elle ne saurait justifier sa conduite en état d'ivresse ;*[4]
– it is used with an interrogative word:
*Elle ne savait quoi lui répondre.*
And when *savoir* refers to something one knows or can do it is normally used with *pas* :
*Vous ne savez pas jouer aux échecs ?*

It must be emphasized that if the deletion of *pas* is associated with informal style (*je sais pas pourquoi il m'ignore*), the use of *ne* without *pas* is associated with a rather formal register (*je ne sais pourquoi*).

Fixed expressions such as *si je ne m'abuse* are often used without *pas*.

*Cet événement, je ne saurais te dire quand il s'est produit.*[5]

## NÉNUPHAR / NÉNUFAR

*L'étang était entièrement recouvert de nénuphars resplendissants.*[6]

The spelling corrections made to French in 1990 recommended reverting to the old way of spelling the word *nénufar*, because of the Arab and Persian origins of the word.

There is always a choice between the traditional spelling and the 1990 corrections, but few people apply the corrections generally. The rule in teaching is not to penalise students when what they write conforms to one or another way of spelling. However, in universities, the trend is to maintain the original spelling and to ignore the spelling changes recommended in 1990.

Monet

4. She wouldn't be able to justify her drunk driving behaviour while she was drunk.
5. I couldn't tell you when this event occurred.
6. The pond was entirely covered with resplendent water lilies.

## NI … NI

*Ni mon frère ni moi ne le comprenions.*[7]
*Il ne parlait ni le français ni l'anglais.*

*Ni…ni* is followed by a plural verb, as the two subjects refer to different people, animals, or objects.

## NIER / RENIER

*Ils ont nié leur culpabilité dans cet assassinat.*[8]
*Ils ont renié leur patrie.*[9]

*Nier* means *to deny*, whereas *renier* is to *renounce* (a faith, an opinion), *to disown* (one's past, one's country), *to break* (one's promise).

## NIGÉRIAN / NIGÉRIEN

*Le président a œuvré pour les relations franco-nigérianes.*[10]

*Les Nigérians* are the inhabitants of *Nigeria /Nigéria*, and *les Nigériens* are those of *le Niger*.

## NONPAREIL

*Sa vertu nonpareille ne peut être que louable.*[11]

This adjective is written as one word.

## NOUS (OF MAJESTY OR MODESTY)

*Nous sommes convaincue de la justesse de cette action.*[12]

If *nous* or *vous* is used as a plural of majesty or modesty, it is considered singular for the purposes of agreement (although there is agreement for gender).

7. Neither my brother nor I understood him.
8. They denied their culpability in this assassination.
9. They renounced their country.
10. The president worked for Franco-Nigerian relations.
11. Her unequalled virtue can only be laudable.
12. We are convinced that this is the right thing to do.

## NOTRE / NÔTRE

*C'est le nôtre.*
*C'est notre frère.*

The forms *nôtre*, *vôtre* (possessive pronouns) are used when they can be replaced by *mien(s)* or *tien(s)*. The forms *notre*, *votre* (possessive adjectives, without the circumflex) are used when they can be replaced by *mon /ma* or *ton /ta*.

If we were applying the rule according to which the circumflex replaces a vowel followed by a silent '*–s*', both words would take a circumflex. *Notre* and *nôtre* both come from Latin *nostrum*.

## NUIRE

*Cet insecte a nui au bien-être de la forêt.*[13]

The past participle does not take a '*–t*', unlike the past participle of *cuire :*

*Ces légumes ont cuit pendant des heures.*[14]

When used pronominally, *nui* is invariable.

*Ils se sont nui en agissant de la sorte.*[15] *Se* is an indirect object here.

## NUL

*Nulle personne ne pense qu'il a raison.*[16] (in general one would say: *Nul ne pense qu'il a raison* or *personne ne pense qu'il a raison*, as *Nulle personne* is redundant).

The *ne* is necessary, and, although it seems to contain the negation, it follows the same rule as *aucun*, *personne*, *rien*, etc.

13. This insect has harmed the natural equilibrium of the forest.
14. These vegetables were cooked for hours.
15. They hurt themselves /each other by acting that way.
16. No one believes he is right.

## Ô

*Ô rage ! ô désespoir ! ô vieillesse ennemie… (Corneille, Le Cid ).*[1]

Ô is an interjection. While it is dramatic, it is nevertheless a natural way to emphasize the sense of what follows.

Why is *'ô'* written with a circumflex?

—Probably to distinguish it from *'oh'* and the letter *'o'* itself.

Corneille

## OBSÉDANT / OBSESSIONNEL

*Obsédant :*

Which obsesses, which imposes itself relentlessly on the mind. Ideas, questions, music are all described as *obsédant* : *Une musique obsédante est récurrente dans tous les films d'Alfred Hitchcock.*[2]

*Obsessionnel :*

Concerned with obsession. *Névrose obsessionnelle* ('obsessive disorder').

Said of someone who suffers from obsession, who displays the symptoms of an obsessive disorder:

*Il avait un besoin obsessionnel de faire le ménage.*[3]

## Œ / Æ

*'Læticia' de Gainsbourg est une véritable œuvre d'art.*

The ligatures *œ* and *æ* are considered single characters. They represent a single sound, similar to *é* (*vitæ*) or *è* (*œstrogène*). This phenomenon has a number of names, including *ligature, lettres soudées, lettres doubles, lettres liées, voyelles liées, oe liés, o-e liés, oe collés, o-e collés, e dans l'o, ligature œ* or *caractère oe ligaturé.*

The letters *'a'* and *'e'* are usually fused when they represent a single sound. This ligature, however, is not obligatory:

1. O rage! O despair! O inimical old age!
2. An obsessive music recurs in all of Alfred Hitchcock's films.
3. He was obsessed with cleaning.

*curriculum vitae* or *vitæ* : the sound *ae* is a diphthong like *oe* (*pœna* from which comes *peine*) and *au* [as in *aurum* from which comes from *'or'* ('gold')].

They remain separate when they form two distinct sounds: *paella*, *aérien*.

Ligatures are never preceded by a *'c'*-cedilla (*ç*). Thus, *et cætera* is written without a cedilla, although it is pronounced *et-sé-té-ra*.

In the Serge Gainsbourg song *Lætiticia*, he sings « *l'e dans l'a* » when spelling the name. When possible, the letters of the alphabet are usually pronounced without eliding the definite article: we say *'le B'*, *'le C'* naturally, but also *'le F'*, *'le H'* even though these start with a vowel sound. This holds also for the pronunciation of the numbers 1 and 11, *'le un'* and *'le onze'*.

A possible reason suggested on a language forum site reads: « *cette prononciation non attestée de Gainsbourg 'l'E dans l'O' est privilégiée par les instituteurs car elle donne une image presque concrète du 'E dans l'eau', aux enfants du CP : 'E dans l'eau', ça ne veut rien dire, mais ça parle aux enfants du CP (surtout si on évoque des 'œufs dans l'eau') en tout cas plus que 'E dans le O'* » (cf. *dans le haut*, but *le haut* of what?).[4]

Comment:

A lot of *'–œ'* sounds are mispronounced: cf. *Œdipe*, *œnologue*, that should be pronounced with /ɛ/ (*'–œ'* is pronounced /œ/ only when followed by a *'u'* cf. *cœur*).

Grevisse and Goosse begin their section on the phoneme known as mute *'–e'* with « *L'[ə] muet, signe de la tendance actuelle, alors que l'on préférerait pour des raisons d'intelligibilité 'le a, le b etc.'* » (Grevisse and Goosse : 1993, 35).

See also under SŒUR.

HITCHCOCK

4. 'This pronunciation, attributed to Gainsbourg, "E in the O" is privileged by teachers as it gives an almost concrete image of "E in the water" to the children in first year of primary school: "E in the water" means nothing, but it speaks to those children (above all if we evoke "eggs in the water", in any case more than "E in the O".'
see http://www.languefrancaise.net/forum/viewtopic.php?id=7651.

## ŒUF

*Puis-je avoir deux œufs pour mon petit déjeuner ?*

*Un œuf* is pronounced /œf/, but the *œufs* in *deux œufs* is pronounced /ø/ (that is, without the final /f/ sound). The same holds for *un bœuf* [ɛ̃bœf] /des *bœufs* [debø].

## OIGNON

*J'ai pelé tellement d'oignons que j'ai les yeux qui pleurent.*[5]

At first, the *'gn'* sound was rendered by *'ign'*. With time, the *'i'* sound disappeared. The changes to French spelling from 1990 propose the spelling *ognon.*

## ON (Agreement)

*On est partis sans rien dire.*

When *'on'* stands for a plural subject such as when it substitutes for the plural *nous*, there is normal agreement for gender and number. This use of *'on'* belongs to a colloquial register.

## ON / L'ON

*L'on était loin d'imaginer un tel succès.*[6]

This usage belongs to a careful, literary register. Originally, grammarians interpreted it as driven by euphony, with the long *'l'* being used to avoid a hiatus between two vowels. The *'on'* is in fact the result of sound change: the origin of *'on'* is in the noun *hom* which derives from Latin *homo.*

We avoid using *l'on* when it would lead to alliteration: *l'on le…*

## ON-DIT

*Il ne faut pas écouter les on-dit ou le qu'en-dira-t-on.*[7]

This noun is invariable.

5. I peeled so many onions that my eyes are tearing (or are watering).
6. Such a success was unimaginable.
7. You should not listen to hearsay or gossip.

## ORANGE

As a colour adjective deriving from a noun, *orange* is invariable: *des ballons orange.*

*Amarante*, *écarlate*, *fauve*, *incarnat*, *mauve*, *pourpre*, and *rose* are the seven exceptions to this rule. These seven are considered to be true adjectives and are pluralized accordingly: *des panthères roses.*

We say *la couleur orange*, or *l'orange* either when referring to the colour itself or to an object of that colour ('the orange one'). *Prends-tu le rouge ou l'orange ?* (but this is not limited to colour adjectives: *prends-tu le grand ou le petit ?*).

*Orangé* ('orangey') takes the mark of the plural, e.g. *des bannières orangées*, except when used as a compound adjective, e.g. *des rideaux orangé vif.*

## ORDER (Syntax)

Ronsard's *Sonnet 18* used the construction S + O + V:

*Une beauté de quinze ans enfantine,*
*Un or frisé de meint crespe anelet,*
*Un front de rose, un teint damoiselet,*
*Un ris qui l'ame aux Astres achemine.*[8]

Ronsard

In *Un ris qui l'ame aux Astres achemine*, the *qui* is the subject of *achemine* : *un ris qui achemine l'ame aux astres.* If the habitual syntactic order is verb + object, one finds an inversion of the object and the verb in poetry and in verse, even if only in order to best place the rhyme or create a certain effect. In Latin, the complement of the direct object was habitually before the verb. In the lyrics of the song by the humorous group *Les Inconnus*, « *Isabelle a les yeux bleus //Isabelle les yeux bleus a* » ['Isabelle has blue eyes //Isabelle (the) blue eyes has'], the inversion is purely ludic and reminiscent of Molière's following passage:

« *Belle Marquise, vos beaux yeux me font mourir d'amour.*

8. 'A childlike beauty just fifteen years old,
The curled gold of so many ringlets
A rosy brow, a maiden's hue,
A smile which carries the soul to the stars.'
(adapted from the translation available on https://oeuvresderonsard.wordpress.com/2012/07).

*Ou bien : D'amour mourir me font, belle Marquise, vos beaux yeux. Ou bien : Vos yeux beaux d'amour me font, belle Marquise, mourir. Ou bien : Mourir vos beaux yeux, belle Marquise, d'amour me font. Ou bien : Me font vos yeux beaux mourir, belle Marquise, d'amour. » (—Le Bourgeois Gentilhomme, Acte I, Scène 4).*[9]

## ORGUE

*Le grand orgue de la cathédrale résonne tous les midis.*[10]
*Les grandes orgues que compte la France font la splendeur du pays.*[11]

Like *amour*, *délice*, and *aigle* (*l'aigle impériale* in heraldry), *orgue* is in theory masculine in the singular and feminine in the plural when it denotes a single instrument.

## ORTOLAN

*L'ortolan est un mets très prisé des gourmets.*

Ortolan is a delicious but outlawed dish, because the bird (a species of bunting) is protected and hunting it is forbidden. The preparation of this dish is most unusual (but considered objectionable by some). The bird is first fattened and then drowned in Armagnac before being roasted whole. President François Mitterrand had it at one of his last meals shortly before his death (and there is a tradition which claims that ingesting the bird with its viscera is a pledge of immortality). The word *Hortolan* was used in the past, as demonstrated by Abbé Féraud's dictionary, but usage without the '*h*' prevailed.

9. 'Beautiful Marquise, your beautiful eyes make me die of love. Or: Love makes me die, Beautiful Marquise, from your beautiful eyes. Or: Your beautiful eyes of love make me, beautiful Marquise, die. Or: To die your beautiful eyes, beautiful Marquise, of love makes me. Or: Make me your eyes die beautifully, beautiful Marquise, of love'.

10. The cathedral's great organ is played at noon every day.

11. The great organs found in France are the country's crowning jewels.

## OS

*Le chien a enterré ses os au fond du jardin.*[12]

According to *Le Petit Robert* and *Le Petit Larousse*, in the singular the '*s*' is pronounced and the '*o*' is open. In the plural, the '*s*' is not pronounced and the '*o*' is closed.

*Des os* is pronounced like *des eaux*.

## OU

(a) If the two subjects are singular and the idea refers to one of the two, the agreement is in the singular:
*Mon frère ou ma sœur viendra avec nous au ciné.*

(b) If the two subjects are singular and the idea refers to the two, the agreement is in the plural:
*La musique ou la littérature lui changeront les idées.*

(c) If one of the subjects is plural, the agreement is in the plural:
*Mon père ou mes beaux-parents seront présents* ('my father or my parents-in-law will be present').

However, in practice, both the singular and the plural are used: *La littérature ou la musique est /sont au programme.* Vaugelas's quote on his deathbed is often used to illustrate these divergences in spoken French: « *Je m'en vais ou je m'en vas, l'un ou l'autre se dit ou se disent* » ('I am going away, one or the other is said or are said'). —Benjamin Legoarant, 1832, p.55.

VAUGELAS

## OUÏR

*Oyez, oyez mesdames et messieurs.*[13]

This verb, which used to be the normal verb for 'to hear' in French (now *entendre*), is now hardly used, except in the second person plural imperative: *oyez*, *oyez*, (cf. English 'hark' or 'hear ye!').

12. The dog buried its bones at the bottom of the garden.
13. Hear ye, hear ye, ladies and gentlemen.

The idiom *être tout ouïe* means 'to be all ears' /'to be listening'. It remains invariable: *il est tout ouïe ; ils sont tout ouïe ; elles sont tout ouïe.*

The phrase *j'ai ouï dire que…* (I had it on hearsay that… /I heard that…) is rather formal and archaic, or used jocularly.

## OURS

*L'ours brun est en voie de disparition dans certains parcs du Canada.*[14]

Since roughly the 13th century, final consonants are not normally pronounced in French. Grevisse gives the example of *drap* which in the plural (and in the singular, too) is pronounced /dra/ (Grevisse and Goosse: 1993, 792). Nevertheless, there are lots of exceptions, in particular words of Latin or other foreign origin, like *campus*, *omnibus*, *prospectus*… *Ours* is an interesting case: the final '*–s*' is pronounced in modern French. Previously, the final '*–s*' was pronounced in the singular but not in the plural. Nowadays, this pronunciation is considered old-fashioned. There is liaison of the /s/ in the form *un ours apeuré.*

In Latin, the singular was *ursus* and the plural was *ursī* (the disappearance of the /s/ sound stems from the fact that the vowel '*o*' was not stressed in Latin and therefore became silent, and the '*s*' disappeared, perhaps through being confused with the first '*s*'). It is highly likely that the 16th-century grammarians then sought to re-establish the final consonants which had been lost from pronunciation.

## OUVRAGE

*C'est un bel ouvrage de couture que tu as réalisé.*[15]

The word *ouvrage* is always masculine. The expression *c'est de la belle ouvrage* is considered non-standard, like the regional phrase *c'est la belle âge.*

14. The brown bear is becoming endangered in several Canadian parks.
15. That's a beautiful piece of needlework that you've knitted.

## PAIR / PAIRE

*Un pair* is a person who is equal to another in a particular domain of expertise, e.g. who carries out the same job (*hors pair* means 'who has no equal' /'peerless', and *aller de pair* means 'to go together' /'go hand in hand'):

*J'en parlerai devant mes pairs.*

*Un individu hors pair, une jeune fille au pair, aller de pair.*

*Une paire* denotes two things or two people which /who are similar:

*Une paire de chaussettes.*

In *jeune fille au pair* there is an idea of economic parity (work in exchange for board and lodging).

See also the homophone PERS.

## PALLIER

*Cette mesure palliera un manque.*[1]

The verb *pallier* requires a direct object complement, and therefore, there is no need for the preposition 'à'. Originally, *pallier* meant *to cover with a pallium* (a coat that the Greeks habitually wore).

## PANTOIS

*Nous sommes restés pantois.*

*Pantois*, which derives from the verb *palpiter* (Rey: 1998, 2550), means 'speechless' or 'dumbstruck'. The feminine form *pantoise* is rare.

1. This measure will compensate for a lack.

## PAON

*Le paon faisait la roue.*[2]

The word *paon* comes from Latin *pavo*, *pavonis*, and is pronounced 'pan' rather than 'pa-on': there is therefore no diaeresis.

## PÂQUES / PÂQUE

*Nous allons célébrer Pâques en mangeant un gigot d'agneau.*[3]
*Pendant la pâque* (with art. & no cap.), *on mange du pain azyme.*[4]

In the 16th century, the plural began to be used to distinguish the Christian festival (*Pâques*) from the Jewish festival (*pâque*). *Pâques* (with no article and a capital) is feminine plural only when used as an epithet, as in: *Joyeuses Pâques*.

## (DE) PAR

*Il voyage de par le monde.*[5]
*Il se croit tout permis de par son statut.*[6]

*Par* is spelled without a '–*t*'.

## PARAÎTRE / SEMBLER

*Il paraît que*: followed by an indicative:

*Il paraît qu'ils sont français d'adoption.*

*Il ne paraît pas que*: normally followed by a subjunctive:

*Il ne paraît pas que la situation soit acceptable.*

*Paraître + adjectif :*

When the verb *paraître* – whether or not it is accompanied by an indirect object – is followed by a predicative adjective, the meaning of the adjective determines the choice of mode. The same holds for *il semble que* [as Grevisse and Goosse note (1993: 1605-1606)].

*Il (me) paraît certain que vous réussirez.*
*Il (me) paraît douteux qu'il vienne.*

2. The peacock fanned out its tail.
3. We are going to eat a leg of lamb to celebrate Easter.
4. At Passover, one eats unleavened bread.
5. He travels around the world.
6. He believes that his status entitles him to do anything.

The 1990 orthographic reform suggested, in the spirit of simplification, the removal of the circumflex accent from the '*i*' of the words *rafraîchir* and *paraître* ; however, this rule is not followed during competitive examinations.

## PARCE QUE

There is no elision when *parce que* is separated by a comma from what follows: *parce que, en ce qui me concerne*, …

Some writers mark elision with *lorsque*, *puisque* and *quoique* only before the personal pronouns *il*, *ils*, *elle*, *elles*, *en*, and *on*. Others always use elision (Grevisse and Goosse : 1993, 53).

See also Car (re difference).

## PARLER (Se)

*Ils se sont parlé pendant des heures au téléphone.*

*Se* is indirect: the past participle remains invariable.

*Je lui parle* : I say something to him/her (*lui* is used for males and females).

*Je parle avec lui* : I converse or discuss with him (for a woman, the expression would be *avec elle*). This latter expression is much less common.

## PAS (Position in the Sentence)

*Je suis désolée de ne pas avoir pu vous aider.*
*Je suis désolée de n'avoir pas pu vous aider.*

The tendency in spoken French, which has an increasing role in the written language, is to place *ne* and *pas* next to each other. It follows that the other construction, with *ne* and *pas* separated, is taking on a slightly more literary nuance. The position of *pas* is a matter of personal choice.

We should not forget that in the expression *ne pas*, as in *ne rien* and *ne personne*, it is the word *ne* which has the negative force: the other word was originally of a different part of speech and can occasionally be omitted when the negation is otherwise evident.

See also Mie, Goutte and Point.

## PASSÉ SURCOMPOSÉ

See Double Compound Tenses

## PASSIVE

*Il fut engagé pour ses qualités de menuisier.*[7]

This example shows a past historic verb in the passive voice, and not a past anterior.

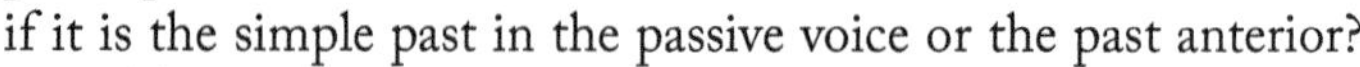

I have the form '*fut* + past participle' and I want to know if it is the simple past in the passive voice or the past anterior?

—Therefore, to elucidate, I replace *fut* with *eut* :

First case: I obtain a grammatically correct form (*il eut engagé*) →
conclusion: my form in '*fut* + past participle' is a simple past in the passive voice.

Second case: I obtain an agrammatical form (*elle se trouva fort dépourvue quand la bise eut venue.*[8]) →
conclusion: my form in '*fut* + past participle' is necessarily a past anterior in the active voice.

*Dès qu'il a terminé ses devoirs :*[9]

In the active voice, the auxiliary *avoir* is used for compound tenses (The subject performs the action of completing: he has finished /did finish /finished the work). With verbs that are not compound, there is obviously no auxiliary : *Le chat mange/mangera /mangerait la souris.*

*Dès que ses devoirs furent terminés :*[10]

In the passive voice, the auxiliary *être* is used.

French has the pronoun *on*, which implies that an active formulation will more readily be used in contexts where English will use a passive: 'he was asked to leave' – *on lui a demandé de partir ;* 'this bed has been slept in' – *On a dormi dans ce lit.*

7. He was hired for his carpentry skills.
8. She [the cicada] found herself sorely deprived when the cold winter wind arrived [correct form: '…*la bise fut venue*'].
9. As soon as he finished his homework.
10. As soon as his/her homework was finished.

## PAST ANTERIOR / PLUPERFECT INDICATIVE

(a) *Dès qu'il avait terminé ses devoirs, il s'en allait.*
(b) *Dès qu'il eut terminé ses devoirs, il s'en alla.*

In example (a), the sense of the pluperfect is 'every time he had finished his homework, he left'.

In (b), the past anterior is 'punctual' and indicates a precise fact. The past anterior belongs to a literary register.

(c) *A peine l'impératrice eut-elle abdiqué qu'il naquit.*[11]

In example (c), the use of the past anterior (*fut né*) or the pluperfect (*était né*) would not be acceptable in this context, as they would express anteriority.

## PAST HISTORIC vs PERFECT

It is not uncommon in newspapers like *Le Monde* to find a verb in the perfect tense and one in the past historic in the same sentence:

*Freud a inspiré … il déclara …*

This would not be recommended in a student essay, for reasons of consistency. The perfect tense in the previous example indicates the continuity of the action or situation up until the present: the past historic on the other hand indicates a past event, considered as a whole, and completed.

It is therefore difficult to interpret this juxtaposition of tenses. We might say that the past historic here indicates a punctual fact. The perfect on the other hand indicates an action whose effects continue after it has been accomplished.

In colloquial French, even in written language, the past historic is usually replaced by the perfect.

Although the past historic is rarely used in speech, it is still occasionally heard. There is no rule against the past historic. It is often used in certain expressions, as in « *ce fut un vrai plaisir* » (the past historic here allows the speaker to avoid a hiatus and the awkwardness of « *ça a été* »). In fact, the past historic of *être* (*fut*) is quite often used. Similarly, we sometimes find the second form of the past conditional: *qui l'eût cru*, *on eût cru.*

11. No sooner had the Empress abdicated, than he was born.

## PAST PARTICIPLE

Agreement or no agreement? Sentence by sentence:

Example 1: *Quelles explications a-t-elle données ?*

The past participle with *avoir* agrees with a preceding direct object.

Example 2: *La leçon que je lui ai donné(e) à étudier* (cf. *je lui ai donné la leçon pour qu'il l'étudie, je lui ai donné à étudier une leçon…*). *Les pages que j'avais donné(es) à lire à François* (cf. *j'avais donné à lire des pages, j'avais donné des pages à lire…*).

The agreement is optional when the pronoun that replaces the direct object can be the direct object of either verb in the sentence.

Example 3: *Les accidents qu'il y a eu.*

*Il y a* is an impersonal expression, so the past participle is invariable.

Example 4: *Ces devoirs, quand je les ai eu terminés.*

– with the double compound past tense.

Here, *terminé(s)* normally agrees. Nevertheless, *Le Littré* points out that it is more natural *not* to make the agreement with the double compound past tense.

Example 5: *Combien de films l'acteur Philippe Noiret a-t-il réalisés ?*

Agrees with the direct object.

When an adverb of quantity accompanied by a complement (as in *combien de périples, trop de jeunes, que de talents*, etc.) is connected to a past participle, the past participle usually agrees with the complement.

Example 6: *Les années que sa vie a duré.*

*Durer* is an intransitive verb without a direct object, so there is no agreement here.

Noiret

Example 7: *Combien d'euros a-t-il payé ?*

– complement indicating quantity, so no agreement.

Compare: *J'ai payé cette voiture 25 000 euros.*

The direct object is *voiture* not *euros*.

Example 8: *Ils ne se sont rien acheté.*

*Rien* is here the preceding direct object. The past participle remains invariable.

Example 9: *Il est des personnages que Balzac a voulus tellement significatifs qu'il les a chargés de valeurs symboliques.*[12]

Grevisse and Goose cite Flaubert: « *Il l'avait rendue fort malheureuse pour se venger* » in *L'Éducation sentimentale* (1993, 1338). Grevisse and Goosse (1993, 1338) add that it is not unusual for this participle (and others) to be left invariable, and this can be easily justified, as we can consider that « *le véritable objet direct est constitué par l'ensemble formé par le nom ou le pronom et son attribut.* »[13]

Personal comment: Balzac did not 'want the characters': rather he 'wanted the characters to be meaningful.' We can therefore accept: *Il est des personnages que Balzac a voulu tellement significatifs qu'il les a chargés de valeurs symboliques.*

Flaubert

## PAST PARTICIPLE + INFINITIVE

Sentence by sentence:

Example 1: *La sonate que j'ai entendu jouer.*

The pronoun *que*, the antecedent of which here is *sonate*, is the direct object of *jouer* only and not of *(ai) entendu*. For this reason, *entendu* is invariable. The direct object of *ai entendu* is, in fact, the (non-explicit but understood) word *quelqu'un* followed by the infinitive and preceded by the past participle: *la sonate que j'ai entendu (quelqu'un) jouer.*

Example 2: *La maison que j'ai vu démolir.*[14]

There is no agreement here. After verbs of perception, an infinitive is normally used. French is not very keen on the passive, just as it is not very keen on adjectives. It favours nouns and active verbs. We would sooner say *on démolit la maison* than *la maison est démolie /est en train d'être démolie. La maison que j'ai vu écraser* contains the idea of 'the house that I saw someone /something demolish', or even 'the

12. There are characters that Balzac wanted to be so significant that he charged them with symbolic values.

13. The true direct object consists of the combination of the noun (or the pronoun) and its attribute.

14. The house that I saw demolished.

house that I saw something demolishing' (with an idea of ongoing action). The idea of having seen the house being demolished is understood but not stated. A French speaker sees straight away that the house is not demolishing itself but that someone or something is demolishing it.

We can say: *J'ai vu la maison reconstruite* (i.e. once it was rebuilt, after it had been rebuilt) and *j'ai vu reconstruire la maison* (i.e. while it was being rebuilt).

N.B.: There is in French no direct equivalent of the English progressive ('I heard him singing'): the same effect is achieved by other means.

In French the past participle implies completion, whereas the infinitive implies ongoing action. Compare the expression « *Le corps que j'ai vu dévoré par les bêtes sauvages* » which implies result, with « *Le corps que j'ai vu dévorer* » (in the process of being devoured).

We can write:

> *Il s'est senti trahi par tous ses amis* (he felt that they had betrayed him, i.e. a state).
>
> *Il s'est senti trahir par tous* (he felt that they were betraying him from all sides, i.e. an action).

The verb *esse* (*être*) had no passive form in Latin. Only transitive verbs had a passive form. There was a construction with an auxiliary in the tenses that we now call 'compound' tenses (such as the past or future anterior): *Amatur* was *il est aimé*; *amatus est* meant *il a été aimé*. The imperfect was *amabar*.

*Janua aperitur* : *On ouvre la porte, /quelqu'un ouvre la porte.*

*Janua aperta est* : *La porte a été ouverte, donc la porte se trouve ouverte* (i.e. a state of affairs).

Example 3: *Cette enfant, je l'ai vu punir.*

The verb *punir* normally takes a direct object; here this is *'l'* which stands for the preceding direct object *cette enfant*: *j'ai vu punir cette enfant.*

Example 4: *Elle s'est senti prendre par la main* (i.e. someone was in the process of taking her by the hand).

*Elle s'est sentie prise par la main* (i.e. She had just been taken by the hand – she had already been taken by the hand). Here the emphasis is on the result of the action rather than on the action itself.

The past participle designates a state which has already been realised. For an action which is in the process of happening, the infinitive is needed.

EXAMPLE 5: *Les soupirants que j'ai envoyés paître.*[15]

AGREEMENT: *que*, standing for *soupirants*, is the direct object of *ai envoyés*. *Paître* is intransitive.

EXAMPLE 6: *La robe que je t'ai vue porter, Delphine.*

AGREEMENT: The direct object *t'* of *ai vu* stands for Delphine and is found before the past participle, while the relative pronoun *que* stands for the noun *robe* and is the direct object of *porter*. However, we would write: *La robe que j'ai vu Delphine porter.*

EXAMPLE 7: *Cette chanson que je t'ai entendue fredonner, Delphine.*[16]

AGREEMENT: The ending *–e* is necessary, but not because of *que* (which stands for *chanson*) which is the direct object of *fredonner*, but because of the *t'* standing for the feminine Delphine. We would write: *Cette chanson que je t'ai entendu* [*sans –e*] *fredonner, Jacques* (masculine noun).

EXAMPLE 8: *Les paroles que je l'ai entendu prononcer.*

The pronoun *l'* is the direct object of *ai entendu*, and the pronoun *que*, standing for *paroles*, is the direct object of *prononcer*. If we were writing about Marie, who is female, we would write: *les paroles que je l'ai entendue prononcer*, with an *–e*. If we were writing about Jacques, who is male, we would write: *les paroles que je l'ai entendu prononcer*, without an *–e*.

EXAMPLE 9: *Je l'ai entendue la lui raconter cette histoire.*

AGREEMENT: This rather weighty expression is correct and is not ambiguous because it tells us to whom the story is told.

– *l'* stands for the person (female) who is telling the story, hence the agreement.

– *la* stands for *cette histoire*.

– *lui* stands for the person (who may be male or female) to whom the story is told.

15. The suitors I have sent packing.

16 That song that I heard you humming, Delphine.

EXAMPLE 10:

*Elle s'est vue accusée* : she found herself in the state of being accused.

*Elle s'est vue accuser* : she suddenly found herself being accused (i.e. people were in the process of accusing her).

EXAMPLE 11:

*La chanson que tu as dit avoir apprise* : *la chanson* is the object of the verb *'apprendre'* and not of *'dire'*.

See also LAISSER.

## PATIENCE

*Elle manque de patience.*

*La patience* means patience in general (cf. *la patience est une vertu* – patience is a virtue), and can be used with a determiner: *Il manque de la patience qui lui serait nécessaire* (what he is lacking is the necessary patience).

*Il manque de patience* simply means 'he is lacking patience'.

## PENDANT / POUR COMBIEN DE TEMPS

*Pendant combien de temps* simply indicates duration.

*Pour combien de temps* indicates an anticipated duration (goal, objective, plan, etc.).

EXAMPLES:

*Pour combien de temps t'étais-tu installé en France ?*

*—Deux ans.*

*Pendant combien de temps es-tu resté en France ?*

*—Deux ans et demi.*

*Depuis la fin du septennat, pour combien de temps le Président, en France, est-il élu ?*[17]

*—Cinq ans.*

By itself, the preposition *pour* serves to indicate a goal.

CHIRAC

17. Since the end of the seven-year term of office, how long is the President elected for in France?

## PENSER

Why do we not say: *je lui pense*, but rather *je pense à lui* –? —We cannot say *penser quelque chose à quelqu'un*. If we were to say *lui penser*, this would be like a complement of attribution, as in *lui donner*. Similarly, we cannot say *lui aller* for *aller à Paris*. [See also PRONOUN.]

The pronoun *lui* before a verb habitually stands for the indirect object, which would have been in the dative case in Latin.

*Lui* comes from *illui*, the dative form of the demonstrative pronoun *ille* in Vulgar Latin.

In *je pense à lui*, *à lui* replaces *ad illum* (in Vulgar Latin) used in place of *de illo* in Classical Latin; it does not replace the dative *illui*. We cannot say *à le*, because *le* is either an article or the direct object.

French has therefore adopted the word *lui* which is the stressed form of the personal pronoun. From Old French onwards, *lui* has been used after a preposition: *J'en ai donné à lui*.

PENSER À /PENSER DE :

*Penser à* : to think about, ponder, imagine.

*Je pense souvent à eux.*

*Penses-y bien.*

*Penser de quelque chose /de quelqu'un* : to have an opinion on, form an idea of something.

We can say: *on en pense.*

*Ce qu'on en pense ne me dérange pas. On n'en pense que du bien.*

## PERFECT / IMPERFECT

*Longtemps je me suis couché de bonne heure.*[18]

The opening sentence of *À la recherche du temps perdu* is in the perfect rather than the imperfect tense. The perfect tense here emphasizes a rupture with the present. The fact of going to bed early is in the past, and it is no longer continuing. The *passé composé* is used here because the narrator takes stock of his past: he looks back and places himself at the moment of enunciation.

18. For a long time, I went to bed happy.

## PERS

*Pers* comes from the late Latin *persus* (= *de Perse*, 'from Persia') meaning blue-coloured[19] [*bleu (couleur tirant sur la pêche)*[20]] and is used to describe a bluey-green colour of eyes in which blue dominates.

*Il a les yeux pers.*[21]

## PERSE / PERSAN

*J'ai appris le persan à l'université.*

The noun *Persan* refers to an inhabitant of Persia after the Arab conquest.

*Le persan* : a language of the Iranian branch, written in Arabic script, spoken in Iran, Afghanistan and Tajikistan.

The noun *Perse* denotes an inhabitant of Ancient Persia, before the Arab conquest.

PERSAN

*Le perse* : the language spoken in the Achaemenian Empire, the ancestor of *persan*.

The adjective *perse* is used in relation to the ancient Persian civilisation.

## PEU

*On attendait de grosses chutes de neige, mais un peu de neige seulement est prévu.*[22]

*On s'attendait à recevoir de la pluie, mais un peu de neige est prévue.*[23]

If the context is about quantity (only a little), *prévu* can agree with *un peu*.

To insist upon the idea that there will be snow, one writes *prévue*.

19. *Glossarium Du Cange*, Paris, 1678 & 1733.
20. *Blaise – Dictionnaire latin-français des auteurs du moyen-âge.*
21. He has blue-green eyes.
22. Heavy snowfalls were expected, but only a little snow is on the forecast.
23. Rain was expected, but a little snow is on the forecast.

## PEUT-ÊTRE (QUE)

Why does *peut-être (que)* not take the subjunctive in French even though it expresses doubt?

—*Peut-être que* does not introduce a subordinate clause. The more polished expression would be *peut-être* followed by inversion: *Peut-être a-t-il réussi.* This construction is often replaced by *peut-être que…* which is often considered to be a Gallicism (*peut-être que c'est lui qui a réussi*).

—*Peut-être* does not take the subjunctive. It is an adverb rather than a conjunction: *Il a peut-être réussi.*

## PEUX / PUIS

*Puis-je* should be used instead of *peux-je* for reasons of euphony.

*Est-ce que je peux* or *est-ce que je puis* are both perfectly acceptable. *Puis* was the form used in Old French. It has been preserved as an archaism in formal expressions: *puis-je* and *est-ce que je puis.*

See also Pouvoir

## PIED

*Nous sommes partis à pied jusqu'à Saint-Jacques-de-Compostelle.*[24]

The noun *pied* remains in the singular, just as *main* remains in the singular in the expression *faire un travail à la main*, even if both hands are used, as well as *ouvrir l'œil*, *fermer l'œil*, *tendre l'oreille*, etc. The expression *à pied* is invariable probably because we advance one foot at a time. *À pied* is opposed to other means of transport such as *à vélo, à cheval*, *en voiture, en train* etc. However, we write *à genoux*, 'kneeling', the two knees resting on the floor.

## PINOT / PINEAU

*Pinot* is a black grape variety grown in Burgundy.

*Le pinot noir.*

*Pineau* is a white grape variety from the Loire.

*Le pineau des Charentes.*

24. We travelled on foot until we reached Santiago de Compostela.

## PIRE / PLUS MAUVAIS

*C'est le plus mauvais gardien de but que j'ai jamais vu.*[25]
*C'est la pire journée de l'année.*

*Le pire /le plus mauvais :*

*Pire* can replace *plus mauvais* when the adjective is not being used with the sense of 'defective'.

In Latin, the words *pejor* and *melior* are comparatives corresponding to *pire* and *meilleur*. *Le pire* was *pessimus* : the same applies to *le meilleur*, which in Latin was *optimus*, not *melior*.

*Dans cette série de vins, indiquez-moi le meilleur et le pire* (the worst here is not necessarily bad).

*Dans cette pile d'examens, quelle est ta meilleure et ta pire note ?* (the worst grade is not necessarily bad in the sense of being inadequate, and the best grade may be low).

## PIS

*La situation va de mal en pis.*[26]

Just as *pire* is the superlative of *mauvais*, *pis* is the superlative of *mal*. Like *bien*, the superlative of which is *mieux*, *pis* is an adverb. A tip for avoiding confusion is to try to replace *pire* by *meilleur* and *pis* by *mieux*.

Note that the contrary of *tant pis* is *tant mieux*.

## PLAIRE (SE)

Like *se rire*, *se plaire* is indirect, so the past participle is invariable. The past participle does not take a circumflex:

*Ils se sont plu dès qu'ils se sont vus.*

The same holds for *déplaire* :

*Ils semblent même s'être déplu la première fois qu'ils se sont vus.*[27]

*Je ferai ce qui me plaît /ce qui me plaira :*

*Je ferai ce qui me plaît :* what I enjoy at the moment and what I will continue to enjoy in the future.

*Je ferai ce qui me plaira* : what I will enjoy at that time in the future, which may be different from what I enjoy at the moment.

25. He is the worst goalkeeper that I have ever seen.
26. The situation is going from bad to worse.
27. They even seem to have disliked each other from their first meeting.

## PLUPART (LA)

*Elle lui donna des conseils dont la plupart étaient excellents.*
*Elle lui donna des conseils dont la plupart était excellent.*

Nowadays, *la plupart* is treated as a plural indefinite pronoun. However, many authors have used a singular verb with this expression.

*La plupart d'entre nous pensent /pensons...*

When the speaker is included in the group, then we would use *pensons*. With a few exceptions, the verb is plural when the object of *la plupart* is plural (*pensent*). Generally, *la plupart* is considered an adverb rather than a noun.

In the first example below the speaker is included in the group; in the second he/she is not:

*(i) La plupart d'entre nous avons voté « oui » au référendum* (i.e. including the speaker).

*(ii) La plupart d'entre nous ont voté « non » au référendum* (i.e. not including the speaker, or at least the speaker is not making it explicit that he/she is included).

## PLUPERFECT SUBJUNCTIVE

The imperfect and pluperfect subjunctives can express hypothetical situations: in a subordinate clause, it is therefore the equivalent of an imperfect or a pluperfect indicative. In a main clause it is the equivalent of a conditional.

Sentence by sentence:

EXAMPLE 1: *Que serait-il devenu, s'il eût perdu la foi ?*[28]

This sentence is elevated and somewhat archaic in style. In modern standard French, we would use the pluperfect indicative: *Que serait-il devenu, s'il avait perdu la foi ?*

EXAMPLE 2: *On eût dit qu'il allait tomber de sa chaise.*[29]

This sentence also is elevated and somewhat archaic in style. In modern standard French, we would use the first form of the past conditional: *On aurait dit qu'il allait tomber de sa chaise.*

28. What would he have become, if he had lost faith?
29. It seemed that he was going to fall from his chair.

EXAMPLE 3: *Il agissait de la sorte, non point parce qu'il est devenu riche et fût devenu vaniteux.*[30]

*Fût devenu* here is a pluperfect subjunctive like the preceding example (which used to be known as the second form of the past conditional). If we replace it with the first form of the past conditional '*…non point parce qu'il est devenu riche et serait devenu vaniteux*', its meaning becomes clearer. His vanity is a real or supposed consequence of his new wealth.

## PLURAL

The '*s*' of the plural in French comes from the accusative plural case in Latin (in the masculine and the feminine: *rosas, dominos, milites, manus…*). Most French nouns come from the accusative case and not from the nominative.

« *Viens mon petit chou sur mes genoux avec tes joujoux et tes bijoux jeter des cailloux sur ce vilain hibou plein de poux* »
– is a mnemonic sentence taught to French school pupils to help them to remember the seven words ending in *–ou* which have a plural ending in *–oux* :
*chou*, *genou*, *joujou*, *bijou*, *caillou*, *hibou*, and *pou*.

The plural in *–oux* comes from medieval manuscripts where a little character was used for '*–us*' that was mistaken for the letter '*x*'. At some point people did not know its origin and started adding another '*u*' that the pronunciation of the word required: *des bijox* (for *bijous*) became *bijoux*.

*Cheval* followed the same process, but the '*l*' was vocalised as '*u*', when an '*s*' was added, as the '*s*' used to be pronounced (*cheval* became *chevauls* and then *chevaux* with '*us*' becoming '*x*').

Actually, the vocalisation of 'l' usually happens when it is followed by a consonant. Generally, the vocalisation is not made in English, unless the borrowing from French was made after the time the '*l*' got vocalised in French.

| | | | |
|---|---|---|---|
| Latin | *falco /-onis* | becoming | *faucon* ('falcon'), |
| | *saltus /-ūs* | becoming | *saut,* |
| | *salsus/a* ('salted') | becoming | *sauce,* |
| | *caldus* (*adj.*) | becoming | *chaud …* |

30. He acted that way, not because he had become rich and vain.

Nouns ending in '–*al*' change '–*al*' to '–*aux*', for example: *le cheval* (*chevaux*), *le bocal* (*bocaux*), *le corail* (*coraux*), *le journal* (*journaux*), *le soupirail* (*soupiraux*), *le travail* (*les travaux*), and *le vitrail* (*vitraux*).

There are a few exceptions, including: *le bal* (*les bals*), *le carnaval* (*les canarvals*), and *le festival* (*festivals*).

Note that the plural of *ail* ('garlic') is *aulx* : *Les étals du marché étaient recouverts d'aulx.*

LES BONAPARTE

Family names are invariable (e.g. *les Sarkozy, les Dupont et Dupond, les Bonaparte*), except when referring to dynasties (e.g. *les Tudors, les Capulets*).

In Latin, it was already the case that the final syllables of words were not stressed, and some were hardly pronounced at all. The plural '–*s*' became silent very early in French. Often the consonant preceding this '–*s*' was itself silent (cf. *bœuf* and *bœufs*, *œuf* and *œufs*, *un os* and *des os*…). There was a lot of uncertainty over this.

The attenuation of final consonants occurred between the 8th and 13th centuries (the '*s*' of the plural and the final '*r*' persisted longer), but this was in a non-uniform manner: some dialects maintained the pronunciation of final consonants.

PLURAL OF WORDS BORROWED FROM ITALIAN:

Some French words are directly borrowed from Italian, which has a different way of signaling the plural form. For this reason, some of them will have a plural form which is similar to the one you would have in Italian, but it is not always the case. It is a matter of usage:

(a) Normally, we write '*des carbonari*', '*des mafiosi*', '*des paparazzi*', '*des tifosi*', as in Italian; but we sometimes find '*des carbonaris*', '*des mafiosis*'.

(b) The plural of the following words normally takes an '–*s*': '*un brocoli*', '*un concerto*', '*un condottiere*', '*un fiasco*', '*un graffiti*', '*un imbroglio*', '*un incognito*', '*un lazzi*', '*un opéra*', '*une pizza*', '*une pizzeria*', '*un scénario*', '*un tempo*', '*un trémolo*'.

(c) The Italian-style plurals of the following words now seem pedantic: *'des concerti'*, *'des condottieri'*, *'des confetti'*, *'des graffiti'*, *'des lazzi'*, *'des scénarii'*, *'des spaghetti'*, *'des tempi'*.

## PLUS

When you can replace *plus* with *more*, there is a full adverbial meaning and it is pronounced /plys/ (*je t'aime plus que lui, il veut plus de sucre dans son café*); if you cannot replace it with *more* it is part of a clitic construction and is therefore pronounced /ply/ (*je ne t'aime plus, il ne veut plus de sucre dans son café*).

In the past, almost all occurrences of *plus* were pronounced as /ply/, but today the pronunciation /plys/ tends to be used in all positive uses, with just a few areas of resistance (notably in the comparative adjective).

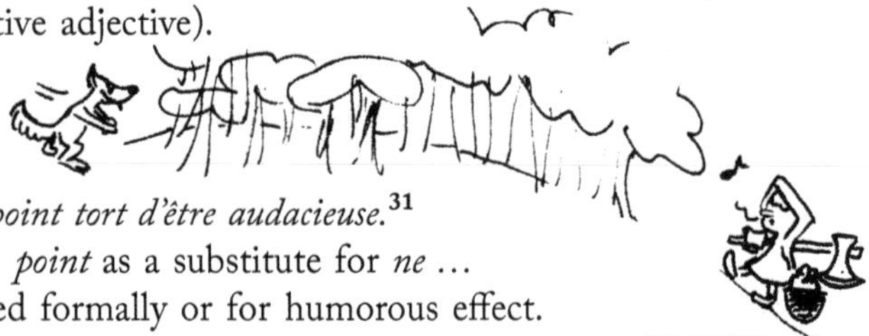

## POINT

*Elle n'a point tort d'être audacieuse.*[31]

*Ne … point* as a substitute for *ne … pas* is used formally or for humorous effect.

LE PETIT CHAPERON ROUGE

## POINTS OF THE COMPASS

When used to designate one position relative to another, these take a lower-case initial letter: *le sud de la Corse.*

One finds *le Sud /sud de la France*, depending on whether it is considered a geographical region in its own right, or as a position relative to the territory of France as a whole.

When they are part of the name of a country or continent, they are capitalised: *L'Afrique du Sud* but *l'hémisphère sud.*

## PORTE-BONHEUR

*Le trèfle à quatre feuilles est un de mes porte-bonheur.*[32]

Invariable compound noun: *des porte-bonheur.* The word is formed from a verb and its complement (*'qui porte bonheur'*). However, we would write *des portes-fenêtres* ('French windows'), as this is formed from two juxtaposed nouns (i.e. several doors and several windows).

31. She is quite right to be bold.
32. The four-leafed clover is one of my lucky charms.

## PORTE-MONNAIE

*Les porte-monnaie fluo sont passés de mode.*[33]

The plural remains invariable (*fluo* also).

## PORTUGAIS

*Elle suivait des cours de portugais le soir à la fac.*

In front of 'a' /'o' /'u', 'g' is pronounced [g], whereas in front of 'e' /'i' /'y', it is pronounced [ʒ] (obviously excluding words of foreign origin…). *Guetter* ('to be on the look-out') is written in order not to pronounce it as *jeter*.

## POURPRE

*Des rivières pourpres.*

*Pourpre* is a colour adjective derived from a noun, but which, as one of the exceptions, follows the normal pattern of agreement.

See Amarante, Écarlate, Fauve, Incarnat, Mauve, Rose.

## POUVOIR

*Pouvoir* in the present indicative: *je peux (je puis), tu peux, il peut, nous pouvons, vous pouvez, ils peuvent.*

*Pouvoir* in the present subjunctive: *que je puisse, que tu puisses, qu'il puisse, que nous puissions, que vous puissiez, qu'ils puissent.*

There is an optative subjunctive: *puissé-je, puisses-tu, puisse-t-il, puissions-nous, puissiez-vous, puissent-ils* (in this form the subject is inverted).

Present imperative *peux* (rare).

*Peux* cannot be used in the interrogative form with inversion of subject and verb: i.e. the correct form is *puis-je*, not *peux-je.*

*Puis* is the first-person form which was phonetically inherited from Latin. This was the only form in Old French. Subsequently, *puis* began to fall out of use and was replaced by *peux*. The form is still used in the present indicative in formal registers (here with *pas* omitted): *Je ne puis saisir la pertinence de cette analyse.*[34] See Peux/Puis-je.

*Puis-je* has the sense of asking permission to do something: *Puis-je vous parler, vous rencontrer ?*

33. Fluorescent wallets are no longer fashionable.

34. I cannot grasp the relevance of this analysis.

## PRÉ

*Quel émerveillement de voir le pré couvert de jonquilles au printemps !*[35]

The word *pré* does not take an '-*s*' in the singular (– occasionally muddled with *près*).

## PRÉMICES / PRÉMISSES

*Les prémices* means 'the beginning'.

*Aux prémices du parlant, le cinéma fit une grande utilisation des techniques du muet.*[36]

In reasoning, *les prémisses* are propositions which start the argument – for instance (a) *Tous les chiens ont 4 pattes ;* (b) *Or mon chat a 4 pattes ;* (c) *Donc mon chat est un chien.*

– (a) and (b) are the *prémisses.*

*Je n'ai pas suivi les prémisses de son argument.*[37]

BUSTER KEATON

## PREMIER

Why do we write: *Elle est passée en premier* (and not *en première*)?

—*En premier* is an adverb, and is therefore invariable, like *primo*, from Latin; which means *au premier rang.*

*En première* would mean *en première classe* (= penultimate year in secondary school, or the first class on a plane or train, depending on the context…).

35. What a marvellous sight, to see the meadow covered in daffodils in the spring!
36. In the early days of sound films, cinema made great use of the techniques of silent cinema.
37. I did not follow the premises of his/her argument.

## PREPOSITION

*Je suis à /dans l'université.*

*'à l'université'* designates the place/location (for example, as opposed to 'at home'). In the larger context of *Mon père n'est jamais allé à l'université*, I am not naming a place, but rather, I just want to say that he did not have a university education. The same is true for *'à l'école'*, *'à l'hôpital'*, *'à l'église'* etc.

*'dans l'université'* means being in the university in the sense of within the university or inside its buildings (being on 'the lawn' of the university does not mean being in the university).

*Je vais à la discothèque /en discothèque.*

*'à la discothèque' :* the first expression refers to a specific club where one habitually goes.

*'en discothèque'* indicates going out at night to a nightclub, without specifying its name /location.

## PRÉSENTER

*On nous avait présenté des excuses.*

The agreement is with the preceding direct object:

(In the masculine) *On nous avait présentés.*

(In the feminine) *On nous avait présentées.*

## PRESENT PARTICIPLE

*Étant malade, elle n'a pas pu venir en classe.*

The present participle on its own expresses the cause, while *en* + present participle does not.

ERRONEOUS USAGES:

The sentence *Tout le monde le dit, comprenant Proust lui-même* is incorrect. Instead, we should write: *Tout le monde le dit* [or, *Tout le monde en convient*], *y compris Proust lui-même.*

Usually the present participle is dependent on a noun or the subject of the action being expressed.

Example: *Se méfiant de tout le monde, Paul n'a pas fait confiance à son meilleur ami.* (i.e. Paul distrusts everyone.)

There is one example of this which was previously criticised but which is now so pervasive that it is commonly accepted. This is the use of *s'agissant de*. Purists recommend instead: *comme il s'agit de...*

Literary Usage:
(see also Aller + Present Participle)

In Verlaine's poem, *Clair de lune*, we find this unusual usage of the present participle:

*Votre âme est un paysage choisi*
*Que vont charmant masques et bergamasques*
*Jouant du luth et dansant et quasi*
*Tristes sous leurs déguisements fantasques.*[38]

With the present participle *charmant*, the poet is expressing a manner of moving. The subjects move, while charming the countryside (which stands for the soul), playing the lute and dancing.

The pronoun *que* here is the direct object of *charmant* : this creates a poetic expression.

Verlaine

## PRESENT / PERFECT

*Il pleut depuis trois jours /Il a plu depuis trois jours.*

Il pleut depuis trois jours implies that it is still raining.

*Il a plu...* implies either that the rain stopped after three days, or that this is a past event (e.g. 'during our holiday, it rained for three days').

Note the difference between: *Cela fait dix jours qu'il pleut*, and *Il pleut depuis dix jours.* The same reality is expressed in both statements, although the latter does not emphasize the duration itself but more the action.

38. 'Your soul is a promised land where
Charming masks and bergamasks bask
Playing the lute and dancing and
Somewhat sad 'neath their fancy masks' [our translation].

## PRÊT / PRÈS

*On n'est pas près de vous oublier.*

*Près de* means *sur le point de* ('about to').

*Il n'est pas prêt à se battre.*

*Prêt à* means *être préparé à* ('be ready to').

## PRÉTENDRE

*Il prétend qu'elle est partie sans payer.*

The verb *prétendre* conveys both opinion and affirmation, and is followed by the indicative (or sometimes by an infinitive).

## PROBABLE / POSSIBLE

*Il est probable qu'il viendra.*

*Il est possible qu'il vienne.*

A probability is concerned with a future event. Therefore, we write: *Il est probable qu'il viendra*, *qu'il va venir.*

We can find the present if it is a present event or situation but the speaker does not know if it is true: *D'après mes calculs il est probable que Pierre et Marie sont en route vers l'aéroport.*

'*Probable*' means that the likelihood of the event occurring is much greater than the opposite scenario.

'*Possible*' simply means that the event may or may not occur.

## PROCHE / PROCHAIN

*Les vacances sont proches.*

*Proche* is the opposite of *loin.*

*Mon prochain examen est en septembre. On espère une paix prochaine au Moyen-Orient.*

*Prochain* implies something that is in the very near future, closest to the present.

## PROMETTRE (SE)

*Elle s'est promis de le faire.*

*Qu'a-t-elle promis ?, que s'est-elle promis ?*

Answer— *de le faire* (the direct object is an expression = *qu'elle le ferait*).

This direct object comes after the verb. The pronoun '*se*' is the indirect object. There is no agreement.

## PRÔNER

*Elle prône toujours la bonne parole.*[39]

This verb comes from the noun *prôsne* (*prosne* in Old French, which meant 'the gate in a church separating the nave from the choir').

Marie Gillain

## PRONOMINAL VERBS

Pronominal verbs can be:

(a) reflexive: *Marie s'est regardée dans la glace.* (i.e. 'at herself').

(b) reciprocal: *Ces coéquipiers se nuisent les uns les autres au lieu de s'entraider dans l'adversité* (i.e. 'each other').[40]

(c) passive in meaning: *Ces marchandises se sont bien vendues* (i.e. 'have been').

(d) without a logical or semantic function, like any other verb (verbs which are purely or essentially pronominal): *Je me souviens de cet évènement.*

(In the last two cases (c) and (d), these were verbs which were formerly reflexive or reciprocal and which have evolved to become completely autonomous like other verbs, but have maintained their pronominal form.)

Sentence by sentence:

Example 1: *Ils se sont brossé les cheveux.*

Here, *se* = reciprocal or reflexive pronoun, which is the indirect object. The direct object comes after the verb.

Example 2: *Ils se sont donné rendez-vous dans le vieux Lyon.*

Here, *donné* is written without an '–*s*' because the direct object (*rendez-vous*) follows the past participle.

Example 3: *Elles se sont rendu compte qu'ils étaient partis.*

*Rendu* here shows no agreement because the direct object (*compte*) follows the past participle.

39. She always preaches the good word.

40. These team-mates harm /undermine one another instead of helping each other in the face of adversity.,

Example 4: *Les cheveux, ils se les sont brossés.*
Because the verb is the reflexive *se brosser*, it takes the auxiliary *être*. The agreement here is with *les*, the preceding direct object.

Example 5: *Ils se sont écrit des lettres.*
*Se* is the indirect object. The direct object, *des lettres*, does not precede the past participle, so there is no agreement.

Example 6: *Les lettres qu'ils se sont écrites.*
The feminine plural direct object, *les lettres*, precedes the past participle.

Example 7: *Elle s'est plainte.*
There is no direct object. The pronoun *s'* is not an indirect object. This is a purely pronominal verb, and so there is agreement with the subject.

Example 8: *Elle s'est demandé pourquoi elle était partie.*
*Pourquoi* here is an interrogative adverb which introduces an indirect interrogative subordinate clause. *S'* is the indirect object.

Example 9: *Elle s'est imaginée victime de la société.*[41]
The reflexive pronoun *s'* is the direct object, and the word *victime* is an attribute of that object. The past participle agrees with the *preceding* direct object.
(cf. *Elle a imaginé elle-même victime.*)

Example 10: *Ils se sont trompés d'heure.*
There is no direct object and the pronoun *se* is not an indirect object. The past participle agrees with the subject. This is not a reflexive verb but a purely pronominal one: it means 'they made mistakes', and not 'they betrayed /deceived themselves'.

Example 11: What is the function of *se* in *Ils se sont vendus comme des petits pains* ?
—*Se* does not have an independent semantic role here. It belongs to the verb (passive in meaning) and can be analysed as part of *se vendre.* Here the past participle agrees with the subject.

41. She saw herself as a victim of society.

There are lots of cases when the nature of the pronoun *se* is unclear as it has gradually lost its semantic function. With transitive verbs (i.e. those that can take a direct object), it seems to retain, at least partly, the character of an indirect object: *Elle s'est acheté une voiture* (where *se* implies 'for herself').

Example 12: *Elle s'est aperçue de son erreur.*

When the pronoun (*me*, *te*, *se*…) in a pronominal verb has no analysable function (that is, when it is neither direct nor indirect object), the past participle agrees in gender and number with the subject. This is a purely pronominal verb (i.e. it only exists in pronominal form). Do not confuse *s'apercevoir* ('to realise'), which is purely pronominal, with *s'apercevoir* ('to catch a glimpse of each other'; « *Elles se sont aperçues au loin* »), which is reflexive or reciprocal.

Example 13: *Elle s'est mariée ce matin.*

*Se marier* is considered to be a different verb from *marier*, because it has quite a different sense: one can *marier* (i.e. 'marry', 'give in marriage') one's daughter or son to someone, whereas one *se marie avec quelqu'un* (i.e. 'marries someone', 'enters into marriage with someone').

In *se marier* the pronoun *se* has no semantic or logical function, being neither a direct nor an indirect object. The past participle therefore agrees with the subject.

Example 14: *Nous nous sommes téléphoné.*

When the pronoun is an indirect object, as is the case here, the past participle of a pronominal verb agrees only with a *preceding* direct object.

If there is no preceding direct object, the past participle does not agree, so *téléphoné* in this example remains invariable.

—[Literal meaning: *Nous avons téléphoné l'un à l'autre /les uns aux autres.*]

Similarly, the past participles of *se rire*, *se plaire* and all of its derivatives such as *complaire* and *déplaire*, *parler*, *se dire* etc. are always invariable.

EXAMPLE 15: *Ils se sont tous les deux appelés Paul.*
Paul is an attribute of the direct object *se*.

EXAMPLE 16: *S'est-elle attendue à un tel succès littéraire ?*[42]
*S'attendre à* ('to wait for one another /each other') is accidentally pronominal: *attendre à* does not exist but *attendre quelqu'un…* does, and the pronoun (*me*, *te*, *se*, etc.) has no semantic function, the participle agrees with the subject.

EXAMPLE 17: *Les troupes françaises se sont emparées de Calais.*[43]
The verb has no direct object, and the pronoun *se* is not an indirect object, therefore the past participle of this purely pronominal verb agrees with the subject.

*Note: Se réveiller* is considered a purely pronominal verb, but originally it meant *to wake oneself up*, as opposed to being woken up by someone else. Nowadays, *se* has become part of the verb and cannot really be analysed. As with *se réveiller*, the verb *se tromper* was originally a reflexive verb before its sense changed.

RECAPITULATION OF AGREEMENT WITH PRONOMINAL VERBS:

(a) When the pronoun is the indirect object (*à qui?*) and the verb has a direct object *before* the past participle, there is agreement with that preceding direct object (*les coups qu'elles se sont portés*).

(b) When the pronoun is an indirect object (*à qui?*) and the verb does *not* have a direct object before the past participle, the past participle is invariable (*ils se sont nui*; *elles se sont porté des coups*).

(c) When the pronoun has no analysable function (i.e. is neither direct nor indirect object), and the verb exists only in pronominal form, the past participle agrees with the subject of the verb (*elle s'est souvenue*, *elle s'est repentie*, *ils se sont doutés de…*).

42. Did she expect such literary acclaim?
43. The French troops seized Calais.

## PRONOMINAL VERBS (ESSENTIALLY OR PURELY)

Essentially or purely pronominal verbs are verbs that are only used in the pronominal form. Without the pronoun, the verb is meaningless. Here are the most common:

*absenter (s')* *abstenir (s')* *accouder (s')* *accroupir (s')*
*acharner (s')* *acoquiner (s')* *affairer (s')* *agenouiller (s')*
*amouracher (s')* *amuïr (s')* *arroger (s')* *autocensurer (s')*
*autodétruire (s')* *autoproclamer (s')* *blottir (se)* *contorsionner (se)*
*contrebalancer (s'en)* *dédire (se)* *déhancher (se)* *démener (se)*
*démerder (se)* *dénuer (se)* *déprendre (se)* *désertifier (se)*
*désister (se)* *dévergonder (se)* *duveter (se)* *ébattre (s')*
*ébrouer (s')* *écrier (s')* *écrouler (s')* *efforcer (s')*
*égosiller (s')* *emparer (s')* *empiffrer (s')* *empresser (s')*
*encanailler (s')* *encorder (s')* *endimancher (s')* *enfuir (s')*
*engouer (s')* *enquérir (s')* *ensuivre (s')* *entraider (s')*
*entredéchirer (s')* *entredétruire (s')* *entredévorer (s')* *entrégorger (s')*
*entremettre (s')* *entretuer (s')* *envoler (s')* *éprendre (s')*
*esclaffer (s')* *escrimer (s')* *évader (s')* *évanouir (s')*
*évertuer (s')* *exclamer (s')* *extasier (s')* *fier (se)*
*formaliser (se)* *gargariser (se)* *gausser (se)* *goinfrer (se)*
*gominer (se)* *gourer (se)* *immiscer (s')* *ingénier (s')*
*insurger (s')* *interpénétrer (s')* *lexicaliser (se)* *lignifier (se)*
*magner (se)* *marrer (se)* *méconduire (se)* *méfier (se)*
*méprendre (se)* *morfondre (se)* *mutiner (se)* *obstiner (s')*
*pâmer (se)* *parjurer (se)* *pavaner (se)* *prélasser (se)*
*rabougrir (se)* *ramifier (se)* *raviser (se)* *rebeller (se)*
*rebiffer (se)* *récrier (se)* *réfugier (se)* *réincarner (se)*
*renfrogner (se)* *rengorger (se)* *repentir (se)* *revancher (se)*
*scléroser (se)* *souvenir (se)* *suicider (se)* *tapir (se)*
*targuer (se)* *toquer (se)* *trémousser (se)* *vautrer (se)*

## PRONOUN

Verbs like *penser, avoir affaire à, être* (in the sense of to belong), *prendre garde, rêver, recourir, songer, renoncer, tenir, se fier, s'adresser* and *présenter quelque chose* are formed with *à* + stressed pronoun when referring to a person.

*Je m'adresse à lui* (but *je lui adresse une lettre*) *; il se fie à elle ; elle pense à eux.* See also PENSER

## PRONOUNS (– Placing of)

Sentence by sentence:

Example 1: In the imperative, we would write:

*Donne-leur du thé /Donne-leur-en /Donne-leur-en, du thé,* or, more commonly, *donne-leur du thé.*

Similarly, we would write: *Donne-m'en.*

Example 2: *Donne-le-moi, ce livre.*

In current practice the direct object comes before the indirect object: *Donne-le-moi.*

The order *donne-moi-le* was previously sometimes found, and is still found, in spoken Canadian French.

## PSYCHIATRE

*Elle voit un psychiatre pour sa dépression.*

The *ch* corresponds to the Greek χ in ψῡχή (*âme*, 'soul') and is pronounced /k/ in French, a '*psychiatre*' being '*le médecin de l'âme*'.

## PUBLIC / PUBLIQUE

*Il est bon public* (used as a noun).

*Il travaille aux relations publiques* (used as an adjective).

The adjective *publique* is the feminine form of *public.*

## PUITS

*Tous les dimanches nous allions chercher de l'eau au puits.*[44]

Cendrillon

*Puits* takes an '*s*' even in the singular. The word comes from the Latin *puteus*. The '*t*' was introduced in the 16th century 'to avoid the homography with *puis*' (our translation of Rey: 1998, 3006), although the word was normally written without, as were its derivations *épuiser* and *puiser*, which gives the noun *puisatier* ('a well-digger').

44. Every Sunday, we used to go to fetch water from the well.

## QUANTITY

*J'écoute de la musique.*
*J'écoute un disque.*

With nouns that designate an indefinite, indeterminate quantity (not countable), the indefinite adjective is used, such as with *air*, *bonheur*, *eau*, *valeur*. In English, the article that introduces an uncountable noun, as in, for example, 'I'm listening to music,' is the zero article /zero determiner.

On the other hand, a countable noun (*disque)* designates (as indicated by its name) entities that can be tallied /counted, and thus put in the plural.

## QUATRE-VINGT(S)

*Il adore la musique des années quatre-vingt(s).*

On the one hand, the absence of the 's' can be justified by saying that it is more about the 'ordinal' value – such as for *page quatre-vingt* which does not take an 's'. On the other hand, the following general rule is applied: the number ends in twenty, and when it is multiplied, it takes an 's'. It will certainly be necessary to wait longer to see which trend will be established and will end up being the required way of doing it.

VANESSA PARADIS

## QUE (ADVERB)

In the sentence *Que d'étudiants a-t-elle envoyés lire la Bible !,*[1] the subjunctive cannot occur after *que.*

*Que* here means 'combien, quel grand nombre' (*Combien d'étudiants a-t-elle envoyés lire la Bible ! Qu'il est grand le nombre…*).

1. The number of students she has sent to read the Bible!

*C'est là que je vis /C'est là où je vis :*

The two structures are acceptable, although the former is of a higher register.

Here are other examples of *que* being used as a pronoun, to replace a relative construction:

*C'est aujourd'hui que le film est projeté.*

*C'est de là que part le ferry pour Cherbourg.*

*C'est dans cette auberge de jeunesse qu'ils sont restés.*

These phrases are all cleft sentences. In order to highlight an element (for example, the adverbial phrase of time in the phrase '*Le film est projeté aujourd'hui*'), a rearrangement is carried out to obtain: *C'est aujourd'hui que le film est projeté.* – *Que* introduces a pseudo relative clause.

## QUÉBEC

*Nous sommes allés au Québec pour les vacances.*

*C'est à Québec que nous nous sommes rencontrés.*

*Au Québec* (the province) is distinguished from *à Québec* (the city).

In Quebec, one constantly hears French spoken as it is spoken in France, in film, in reports, with artists, even in films and documentaries which are dubbed in France, without forgetting the news and TV5. In the network of information from Radio Canada, the Journal of France 2 is presented at least twice a day. This creates a certain standardization.

It is essentially the ancient influences of the English language which have resisted for the longest possible time, because they often date back from the time of the British colonization of the American hemisphere.

People say *bienvenue* when one thanks them, which does not prevent others from saying *je vous en prie* and so on. If one still hears people say *bonjour* (translated literally from 'good day' /'have a good day'), one hears more often people say *bonne journée, bonne fin de journée.*

## QUEL

*Quelle ne fut pas sa joie de le revoir après tant d'années !*[2]

Exclamative adjective which agrees with the following noun.

## QUELQUE

Invariable when used adverbially.

(a) Adverb meaning *environ*:

*Il y a quelque cinquante personnes dans la salle.*

(b) Adverb of quantity followed by an adjective:

*Quelque intelligents qu'ils puissent être, ils ne sont pas doués en maths.*[3]

## QUEL QUE

*Je n'accepterai aucune concession quelle qu'elle soit.*[4]

Written as two words, and agreeing with the following noun.

*Quelle que soit la raison de son acte /quelle qu'en soit la raison, je ne comprends pas.*[5]

In the first expression, the complement is explicit (*la raison de son acte*). In the section expression, the complement is expressed by the pronoun '*en*' which means 'of that /of this reason.'

## QUELQUE CHOSE

*Ce n'est pas quelque chose de grave, ne t'inquiète pas.*

Written as two words and used as masculine, unlike *chose*. See also Rien De.

## QU'EN-DIRA-T-ON

A noun, meaning 'the opinion of others' /'what others say'.

*Il ne faut pas se fier au qu'en-dira-t-on.*[6]

2. How overjoyed she was to see him again after so many years!
3. No matter how clever they may be, they are not gifted in maths.
4. I will not accept any compromise, no matter what it may be.
5. No matter what the reason is for his action /for whatever reason, I don't understand.
6. One should not care about what other people will say.

## QUI (Distributive)

*Chaque habitué apportait qui sa canne, qui son manteau, qui sa lanterne* (—Balzac, *La Vieille Fille*).[7]

In this rather archaic formulation, *qui* is necessarily repeated, at least twice, in order to separate and individualize the different parts of a whole. (See Riegel & al 1994: 212).

Honoré de Balzac

## QUICONQUE

*Quiconque enfreindra la loi sera puni.*[8]

Quiconque means anybody who has done, who will do, or would really do it.

This is not about potential, about someone who could find himself/herself in a given situation, but of any person who had been, is, will be or would be concerned by the action in question.

The verb can also be in the passive voice:

*Quiconque a été nommé (en fait) doit se présenter…* ['Whoever was appointed /named (in fact) must present him or herself…']

Even the conditional indicates a fact that could be real: *Quiconque ne respecterait pas cette règle serait puni* ('Anyone who fails to respect this rule…).

## QUI SOIT / QU'IL SOIT

Depending on the meaning, we can write: *Les paysans, les plus pauvres qui soient* (i.e. 'the poorest of the peasants', 'the poorest we might think of').

*Les paysans si pauvres qu'ils soient…* (i.e. 'the peasants, despite the severe poverty they might be suffering…' /'however poor they are…').

We can also write: *Les paysans les plus pauvres qu'il y ait.*

7. Each regular customer came, one with a cane, one with a coat, the last with a lantern.
8. Whoever breaks the law will be punished.

## QUOIQUE / QUOI QUE

*Quoique*, written as one word, means *bien que* (and has a somewhat more literary register); and written as two words when it means 'whatever':

*Quoiqu'il dise la vérité, je ne lui fais pas confiance.*

*Je ne le crois pas quoi qu'il dise.*

RAIPONCE

## RAIPONCE

*La raiponce aurait des vertus médicinales insoupçonnées.*[1]

A well-known trap in *Les Dictées de Bernard Pivot*. A homophone of *réponse*, *la campanule raiponce* is a plant, the root and flowers of which are used as a vegetable and in salads.

It is also the title of a fairy-tale by the Brothers Grimm (*Rapunzel* in English).

## RAPLAPLA

*Ils sont raplapla à force de veiller la nuit.*[2]

This adjective, a reduplicative form of the onomatopoeic '*pla*', is invariable.

## RAPPELER (SE)

*Je me rappelle qu'il a pris le train pour Ajaccio.*

*Je ne me rappelle pas qu'il ait pris le train pour Ajaccio.*

*Se rappeler* functions like '*penser*' or '*croire*'. The subjunctive is used in clauses introduced after verbs of opinion, affirmation, and perception, when these verbs are in the negative or interrogative forms.

Note the nuance in familiar French:

*Je ne me rappelle pas qu'il soit venu* = 'I don't know if he arrived: perhaps he arrived, perhaps not, I do not recall.'

*Je ne me rappelle pas qu'il est venu* = 'He arrived, they tell me, but I do not recall.'

*Il se rappelait d'elle comme d'une femme désagréable* : The second '*d*' has the same meaning as the first, but it marks the woman's rapport with the implied verb. He remembered her as he remembered a disagreeable woman.

1. Rampion bellflowers are said to have unexpected medicinal properties.
2. They are shattered from staying up all night.

This sentence is rather colloquial and one would favour the structure:

*Il se souvenait d'elle comme d'une femme désagréable.*

See '*se rappeler quelque chose*' versus '*se souvenir* **de** *quelque chose*' *under* SOUVENIR (SE).

## RENDRE

*Se rend-il en France cet été ?*

The silent '*d*' in liaison with a vowel forms a '/t/' sound, as in *prend-il ses affaires?* When the verb ends in '*–te*' or in '*–e*', there is a euphonic '*t*' in the written form, surrounded by hyphens:

*Habite-t-il à Nice ? ; Mange-t-il sa soupe ?*

A note on the pronunciation of *rend-il*, *prend-il* :

All verbs in Latin ended in '*t*' in the third person singular, e.g.:

| | |
|---|---|
| *amat* | ('*aime-t-il*'), |
| *cantat* | ('*chante-t-il*'), |
| *vadit* | ('*va-t-il*'), |
| *prehendit /prendit* | ('*prend-il*'), etc. |

The final vowel (the second '*a*' in *amat*, or the '*i*' in *prehendit*, etc.) was dropped from pronunciation before the 11th century, while the '*t*' was still being pronounced as the final phoneme, before ultimately disappearing itself. The euphonic '*t*' is simply used to avoid an unwanted hiatus.

## RENDRE COMPTE (SE)

*Ils se sont rendu compte de leurs erreurs.*

The past participle is invariable.

The '*se*' is indirect: *rendre des comptes à quelqu'un.*

## RÉSIDANT / RÉSIDENT

*En résidant en France, il a beaucoup amélioré son français.*[3]

*Les résidents du cinquième sont très bruyants.*[4]

The former is the past participle formed with *avoir* and is therefore always invariable; the latter is a noun.

3. His French improved greatly from living in France.
4. The inhabitants of the fifth arrondissement are very noisy.

## RÉSOUDRE

*La question a vite été résolue.*

Résolu is the past participle of *résoudre.*

## RESSEMBLER

*Que d'événements qui ont traversé l'histoire de France se sont ressemblé !*[5]

Invariable: '*se*' is indirect.

## RÉUSSIR

*Il a réussi ses examens avec brio.*

*Réussir à* is normally followed by a verb. With the preposition (*réussir à un examen*), the speaker emphasizes the exam itself rather than the process of passing.

## REVANCHE / VENGEANCE

*La vengeance est un plat qui se mange froid.*

*J'ai pris ma revanche.*

*Une revanche* is for a game ('return game'). *Prendre sa revanche* for the one who loses.

*Une vengeance* means harming others to take revenge for the evil that one has suffered.

*Se revancher* is an archaism sometimes used in a literary context.

## RÉVEIL / RÉVEIL-MATIN / RÉVEILLE-MATIN

*Les trois réveille-matin se sont mis à carillonner en même temps.*[6]

The compound noun *un réveil-matin /un réveille-matin* is (generally[7]) invariable in the plural: *des réveille-matin,* while *réveil* is variable: *des réveils.*

5. Many events which have occurred throughout the history of France echo one another!
6. The three alarm clocks started to ring at the same time.
7. The 1990 spelling reform accepts a variable plural.

## RÊVER

*À quoi rêves-tu ? Je rêve à toutes les possibilités que m'apporterait une telle expérience linguistique.*[8]

*Rêver à :* 'To dream about' – to have one's mind occupied by a thought while being detached /removed from reality.

*Rêver de :* To dream of something while sleeping:
*J'ai rêvé d'elle ; j'ai rêvé que je parlais en français.*

*J'y rêve* (rare): I think about something and I examine the possibility of obtaining it (example: when I was a child, I had already dreamt about having a career in medicine).

*J'en rêve :* I strongly desire something and this idea is constantly in my mind.

## RIEN DE

*Il n'était pas gras, mais extrêmement bien nourri ; ses joues étaient rebondies, et sur la couverture kaki reposait une main vulnérable qui n'avait rien de rugueux.*[9]

*Rugueux* here relates to *(ne) rien*, a neutral pronoun, which follows the normal masculine agreement.

The expression *quelque chose* is likewise followed with a masculine: *Sa façon de parler a quelque chose de séduisant.*

## RIME NORMANDE

Some poets make a rhyme from words which have the same spelling but differ in whether the final consonant is pronounced (as in *mer)* or silent (as in *aimer*). This is known as *rime normande*, because this is the normal pronunciation in Normandy.

In Baudelaire's *Correspondances*, *aimer* is pronounced /emɛr/:

*Elle était donc couchée et se laissait aimer,*
*Et du haut du divan elle souriait d'aise*
*À mon amour profond et doux comme la mer.*

This is also known as *rime pour l'œil* ('eye-rhyme'), because poetry is only rarely read aloud.

8. I am dreaming about all the possibilities that such a linguistic experience would bring me.
9. He was not fat, but extremely well fed; his cheeks were well-rounded, and a vulnerable hand with no trace of wear was resting upon the khaki blanket.

## RIRE (SE)

*Ils se sont ri de ses aventures.*

Invariable: *se* is indirect.

*Rie*, *ries*, *rie*, *riions*, etc. is the subjunctive present conjugation of *rire*.

CRUSOÉ

## ROBINSON CRUSOÉ

*J'ai toujours été fasciné par les aventures de Robinson Crusoé.*

Written *Robinson Crusoé*, with an acute accent on the *'é'*. Compare *canoë*, with a diaeresis, and *canoéiste* – a reason given for the difference is that *Crusoé* first appeared in French in 1720, whereas *canoë* (with initial variations *canoé*, *canoe*) entered the language in the late 19th century, by which time the spelling of *Crusoé* was already established.

## ROLLED /R/

There are three distinct types of /r/ in French, as has been indicated by Alex Vanneste, Professor of French language at the University of Antwerp (adapted from Vanneste : 2005, 144):

(a) The rolled /r/ is called the apical /r/ because it is produced by a vibration of the point – the apex – of the tongue. This rolled /r/ is characteristic of the pronunciation of meridional speakers, especially at the level of familiar, popular, and current language.

(b) The 'Parisian' /r/ is produced by a very light rubbing at the level of the pharynx (pronounced at the back of the mouth, barely audible).

(c) The uvular trilled /r/ also called *grasseyé* in French is produced by a vibration of the uvula.

'If the rolled /r/ is very common in the south,' Alex Vanneste highlights, 'it also appears in other regions of France, but it is equally very common in a popular or familiar register in the north of France, in Burgundy, in Wallonia (Belgium), and in certain rural areas. The rolled /r/ is thought to be the /r/ most employed in France until the XVI-XVII centuries' (—private communication: January 2014).

Needless to say, as far as idiosyncratic pronunciations of the rolled /r/ are concerned, there are differences from one individual to another. However, these slight phonetic differences are barely perceived by most speakers, and are, thus, assimilated to the same phoneme (with the same distinctive or phonological function).

The Parisian /r/ can be heard in some recordings of popular speech of the 1930s (in films with Jean Gabin for instance, with a pronunciation reconstituted by the actors). Linguist Philippe Martin, in an email (private communication, January 2014), lets us know that in recordings of the national assembly in the 1910s, this /r/ was barely pronounced. The trilled uvular /r/ which can be heard in popular songs of the 1930s was not, as commonly thought, a lower-class feature of the Ménilmontant[10] dialect, but belonged to the singing tradition and can still be found today in opera singing.

According to Alex Vanneste, the way Maurice Chevalier, Claude Nougaro, and Edith Piaf, for example, pronounced the /r/ is slightly different and can vary from one song to another.

Many singers used the rolled /r/ because it is more resonant than the Parisian /r/ (which is barely audible). Piaf often used the trilled uvular /r/ (*La vie en rose*), while Chevalier used the apical /r/. Jacques Brel's /r/ (as in *Ne me quitte pas*), like that of Charles Aznavour, was equally trilled uvular, except from time to time at the end of a word, where it was practically Parisian. In Charles Aznavour's *Plus beau que tes yeux* /'More Beautiful Than Your Eyes' (1951), a Parisian /r/ and a trilled uvular /r/ are heard alternatively, depending upon the phonetic context. The /r/ of Luis Mariano (of Franco-Spanish

Aznavour

10. In the 20th arrondissement of Paris.

origins) is rolled (as in *C'est magnifique*). In *Valentine*, the /r/ of Chevalier is typically rolled.

As for the French philosopher Gaston Bachelard's unique pronunciation, at an old age, he used a slightly trilled apical /r/, alternating with a Parisian /r/ (—adapted from a private communication: January 2014).

CHEVALIER

The rolled letter 'r' has always been devalorized in Quebec, even if, in the olden days, it was often heard in some societies. The letter 'r' was still pronounced with a roll in Quebec before the 1960s:

« *Il y avait ce qu'on appelait le 'cours classique' enseigné dans les collèges, et les professeurs (surtout religieux) roulaient le 'r'. Donc, les élèves apprenaient à parler ainsi.* »[11]

## ROSE

The adjective *rose* is a colour adjective derived from a noun, but it is one of the exceptions which therefore agrees normally: *des flamants roses* ('flamingos').

See AMARANTE, ÉCARLATE, FAUVE, INCARNAT, MAUVE, and POURPRE.

11. 'There was what was called the "classic course" taught in the colleges, and the professors (mostly religious) did roll the "r". Therefore, their students learned to speak that way.'
See http://www.sceptiques.qc.ca/forum/le-quebecois-roule-t-il-le-r-mythe-ou-realite-t9802.html

## –S

The 's' of the second-person singular present indicative comes from the original Latin form: *cantas* became *tu chantes*.

'S' became mute from the 18th century, and 's' became a predominantly written feature, with only a few exceptions: *mœurs*, *tous* (Grevisse and Goosse: 1993, 792). See PLURAL

## SABLER / SABRER

*Sabler le champagne* means to drink champagne for a happy occasion.

*Sabrer le champagne* means to remove the cork (and neck) with a sword.

## SAINT-EXUPÉRY

*Le Petit Prince de Saint-Exupéry est l'une des œuvres qui ont marqué mon enfance.*[1] – Written with a hyphen.

The first fifty-franc notes to be issued from 1992 to 1993 contained an error in having an accent on the first *e* of Saint-Exupéry – this led to great controversy in France.

SAINT-EXUPÉRY

## SANS

*Un gâteau sans œuf /Un gâteau sans œufs.*

Both usages are acceptable. However, logically one would rather write '*sans œufs*' (plural). One normally uses more than one egg to make a cake (compare *un gâteau avec un oeuf* with *un gâteau avec des oeufs*).

1. Saint-Exupéry's *Le Petit Prince* is one of the most memorable books from my childhood.

## SANS QUE

*Ils sont partis sans qu'il sache pourquoi.*[2]

*Sans*, from the Latin *sine (si ne)*, is negative. The *ne explétif* should be avoided after the expression *sans que*, although *sans qu'il ne sache* is common usage.

## SATIRE / SATYRE

*L'auteur se livre à une satire virulente de la société de son temps.*[3]

*Une satire* is a work which attacks someone or something by satirising it.

*Un satyre* is a mythological being which is half-man, half-goat:

*Le dieu Pan apparaît dans les tableaux de Lorrain sous la forme d'un satyre.*[4]

## SAUPOUDRER

*Saupoudrer le gâteau de sucre glace avant de le déguster.*[5]

Originally meant *poudrer en versant du sel* (from Latin *sal*, 'salt').

## SAVOIR / CONNAÎTRE

*Il connaît /sait le français.*

With *connaît*, this means that he has a good knowledge of French, at least theoretically.

With *sait*, it means that he has this knowledge and can use it.

*Je l'appellerai dès que je saurai /connaîtrai l'adresse.* These have very similar meanings –

*Dès que je saurai* = 'when I am no longer ignorant of';

*je la connaîtrai* = 'when I have learned /come to know.'

## SAVOIR GRÉ

*Nous vous saurions gré de bien vouloir donner suite à notre demande.*[6]
We write *nous vous saurions gré*, as it comes from the infinitive *savoir gré*.

2. They left, without him knowing why.
3. The author indulges in a searing satire of his contemporary society.
4. The god Pan is depicted in the form of a satyr in Lorrain's paintings.
5. Sprinkle the cake with icing sugar before serving.
6. We would be grateful if you followed up on our request.

## SECOND / DEUXIÈME

*Ils ont combattu côte à côte lors de la Seconde Guerre mondiale.*[7]

We use *seconde* for the second of two, and *deuxième* for the second of more than two.

At the present time there have been only two 'world' wars. Some people therefore prefer to speak of *la Seconde Guerre mondiale*. However, the word *second* comes from the Latin *secundus* which means 'second of two, three, four, five, etc.'

If there were to be a third world war, we would then talk about *la Première Guerre mondiale*, *la Deuxième Guerre mondiale* and *la Troisième Guerre mondiale*.

**SEMBLER :** See PARAÎTRE

## SEMBLER QUE

The mood which follows *il semble que* depends on the degree of probability:

(a) When it means *il est très probable que*, it takes the indicative or the conditional if it is followed by a *si* clause: *Il semble qu'il va faire froid* ; *il semble qu'il partirait si on ne lui offrait pas ce poste.*

(b) When it means *selon les apparences* ('apparently'), it takes the subjunctive: *Il semble que sa promotion soit envisageable.*

*Il ne semble pas que /Semble-t-il que* (in the negative or interrogative) is normally followed by the subjunctive or conditional:

*Il ne semble pas qu'il dise la vérité ;*
*il ne semble pas qu'il serait plus heureux, s'il gagnait au loto.*

*Il me [te, lui…] semble que* (with a pronoun and in the affirmative) is normally followed by the indicative or the conditional:

*Il me [te, lui…] semble que cette remarque est appropriée.*

*Il me [te, lui…] semble que* (with a pronoun and in the negative or interrogative) is normally followed by the subjunctive:

*Il ne me [te, lui…] semble pas que cette remarque soit appropriée.*
*Te semble-t-il que cette remarque soit appropriée ?*

7. They fought side by side in the Second World War.

## S'ENDORMIR / DORMIR, S'ENFUIR / FUIR, S'ENVOLER / VOLER

*Je me suis endormi à minuit /Il dort comme un bébé.*
*Il s'est enfui de prison /Le bruit a fait fuir tous les animaux.*
*Les oiseaux se sont envolés à l'approche du bateau /L'avion vole au-dessus de l'océan Atlantique.*

Compare –
*Il dort :* he is actually sleeping;
*il s'endort :* he is falling asleep.
*Il fuit*: he performs the action of fleeing – he is in the midst of escaping /of evading (he runs, he flees);
*il s'enfuit :* he *begins to* flee, he begins to escape /to evade (he runs away).
*Il vole :* he is in the midst of flying;
*il s'envole :* he leaves, he *starts to* fly, he goes…

## SEOIR

*Cette robe sied à ravir à la mariée.*[8]
*Elle portait un chemisier qui lui seyait fort bien.*[9]
This verb is very rarely used.
See SEYANT and SIS(E)

## SÉPARER

*Elle a vécu pendant des années avec Corentin et s'est finalement séparée de lui.*[10]

We tend to write *elle s'est séparée de lui* rather than *elle s'en est séparée*. However, we find the following in the French *Huffington Post* : « *Garder MAM (Michèle Alliot-Marie, ministre des Affaires étrangères) ou s'en séparer : le casse-tête de Sarkozy* » (24 February 2011).[11] *En* here is used for a person.

8. This dress suits the bride marvellously.
9. She was wearing a blouse that was very becoming.
10. She lived with Corentin for years, before finally separating from him.
11. http://archives-lepost.huffingtonpost.fr/article/2011/02/24/2416088_garder-mam-ou-s-en-separer-le-casse-tete-de-sarkozy.html

## SEUL

*Seuls les Français aiment autant le fromage de chèvre.*[12]

When *seul* means *uniquement*, it has an adverbial function but still agrees in gender and number. *Eux seuls aiment…* would be more emphatic. When the adjective is nominalised, we write:

*Étant les seuls à le faire, les Français… Les Français sont les seuls à manger la tête de veau…*

… DES CUISSES DE GRENOUILLE.

## SEYANT / SÉANT

*Cette robe est seyante.*

*Seyant*, the modern form of the verb *seoir*, means 'qui va bien', 'qui avantage'.

*Séant* means 'qui est convenable', 'qui est décent' :

*Il ne serait pas séant de partir maintenant.*[13]

Not to be confused with the homonym *céans* ('here', which in the following example means 'inside the building in which the speaker currently is'):

*Nous mangerons céans.*

## SI

Hypothetical '*si*' clauses are composed of two parts:

| 'Protasis' and | 'Apodosis': |
|---|---|
| *Si tu étais belle,* | *je t'aimerais davantage.*[14] |
| SUBORDINATE CLAUSE & | MAIN CLAUSE |

(a) *Si* + Present /Future in the main clause –
The hypothesis concerns the future, the condition can be realised:
*S'il fait beau demain, j'irai jouer au tennis.*

(b) *Si* + Imperfect /Conditional in the main clause –
The hypothesis concerns the future, the condition has little chance of being realised:
*S'il faisait beau demain, nous irions jouer au tennis.*
Or – the hypothesis concerns the present, the condition cannot be realised:
*S'il faisait beau, nous irions jouer au tennis.*

12. Only the French show such fervour for goat's cheese.
13. It would be unfitting to leave now.
14. If you were beautiful, I would love you more.

(c) *Si* + Pluperfect /Past conditional –
The hypothesis concerns the past, the condition was not realised:
*Samedi dernier, s'il y avait eu moins de pluie, nous serions allé(e)s nous promener dans le parc.*[15]
(The condition was not realised: there was a lot of rain.)
Compare:
*Si j'étais un homme riche, j'aurais acheté une villa.*
= If I were a rich man, I would have purchased a villa.
and
*Si j'avais été un homme riche, j'aurais acheté une villa.*
= If I had been a rich man, I would have purchased a villa.
– The verb is given the value of a state (in the first phrase), but not the meaning of whether I were rich at that moment back in time (in the second phrase).

Other combinations (when the subordinate clause expresses a fact prior to the principal clause):

(d) Si + passé composé /present in the main clause –
*Si tu as fini tes devoirs, tu peux aller jouer.*

(e) Si + passé composé /future in the main clause –
*Si la fièvre n'a pas baissé demain, tu iras voir le docteur.*[16]

(f) *Si* + Pluperfect /Conditional in the main clause
*Si je n'avais pas acheté ce pull en solde, je le rendrais.*[17]

(g) *Si* = *quand, chaque fois que* –
*S'il pleut, nous jouons du piano en vacances.*
In the past:
*S'il pleuvait, nous jouions du clavecin en vacances.*[18]

15. Last Saturday, if there had been less rain, we would have taken a walk in the park.
16. If the fever has not gone down tomorrow, you will go and see the doctor.
17. If I had not bought this jumper on sale, I would return it.
18. If it rained, we played the harpsichord while on vacation.

(h) *Si…et si…* = *Si…et que…* (literary) –
*Si vous annulez un voyage et si vous ne prévenez pas la compagnie, on ne vous remboursera pas.*[19]
*Si le brouillard persistait et que l'avion ne puisse décoller, il vous faudrait passer une nuit sur place.*[20]
– The choice of the subjunctive belongs to a more formal register; in a more colloquial register one would say:
*Si le brouillard persiste et que l'avion ne peut pas décoller.*

(i) There can be a Conditional after '*si*' :
*Je ne savais pas si j'aurais terminé.*[21]

It should be noted that this is an exception. In this sentence, the 'if' is not an 'if' of condition /hypothesis (= 'if'), but an 'if' of alternative /opposition (= 'whether'), which is why a conditional can be used – and which is here 'a future in the past', i.e. *Je ne sais pas si j'aurai terminé* becomes *Je ne savais pas si j'aurais terminé.*

However, the canonical rule "'ifs' don't like '–rais'"[22] remains largely valid, and makes it possible to avoid statements such as 'si j'aurais su…' This is an indirect interrogative subordinate clause and the direct object of *savais.*

## SI BIEN QUE / DE SORTE QUE

*Si bien que* is considered partially like an adverbial phrase of manner and is therefore followed by the indicative.

When *si bien que* is used, the idea is that a cause has been carefully put in place to lead to a particular result:

*Réfléchissez toujours avant d'agir si bien que vous réussirez presque toujours ce que vous entreprenez.*[23]

19. If you cancel a vacation and if you don't inform the company, we will not reimburse you.
20. If the fog persisted and the plane couldn't take off, you will have to spend a night there.
21. I did not know if I would have finished.
22. « *Les 'Si' n'aiment pas les '–rais'* »
23. Always think before acting, and you will nearly always succeed in your endeavours.

*De sorte que* is used either with the indicative (when a consequence is considered to have occurred) or the subjunctive (when there is an idea of a goal in addition to the idea of an unrealised consequence).

*Ce pays est intervenu de sorte que la paix est préservée* (actual consequence).[24]

*Je travaille de sorte que nous puissions nous payer des vacances* (unrealised consequence).[25]

## SINGULAR / PLURAL

*La Peste de Camus est l'une des œuvres qui ONT marqué mon enfance.*[26]

The relative subordinate clause is the complement of the noun *œuvres*, which is in the plural. The verb *marqué* (whose subject is *qui*, whose antecedent is *œuvres*) is in the plural.

Camus

*Maxime ou Hugo sera premier de la classe.*

When the conjunction of coordination *ou* coordinates two terms which exclude one another, the verb bears the mark of the singular. It is either *Maxime* or *Hugo* and not both.

See Ou.

## SIS(E)

*Cette maison sise à Plougastel est très jolie.*

Past participle of *seoir.*

24. This country intervened in order to maintain peace.
25. I am working so that we can afford a holiday.
26. *The Plague* by Camus is one of the works that had marked /that did mark /that marked my childhood.

## SIX

*Il y a six enfants dans la cour de récréation.*[27]

Is *six* pronounced /si/ or /siz/: *six personnes* ?

—The normal rule is: /si/ *personnes*, but /siz/ *enfants* (/si/ is used in front of a consonant, and /siz/ in front of a vowel).

When *six* is not a determiner, it can be and often is pronounced /sis/ [e.g. *Combien as-tu de cousins ? – J'en ai six* (/sis/)]. The same will be true for *dix*.

Formerly, the *'f'* in *neuf* and the *'t'* in *sept* were not pronounced before a consonant; today, however, the *'f'* and the *'t'* are both pronounced in these contexts.

## SŒUR

*Je suis allé rendre visite à ma sœur.*[28]

In French, the œ signals the Latin or Greek origin of a word. The ligature œ is pronounced differently than oe. Words of Latin origin (for instance, *cœur* from *cor*, *œil* from *oculus*, *œuf* from *ovus*, and *sœur* from *soror*) are pronounced /œ/ or /ø/, while words of Greek origin like *fœtus* or *Œdipe* are pronounced /e/.

See also Œ.

## SOI / LUI

*Soi* comes from the reflexive pronoun 'se' in Latin. *Il*, *elle*, etc. come from the pronoun and the demonstrative adjective 'ille, illa, illud'.

With a specific subject, *lui* or *elle* is employed: *Mon frère avait en lui / ma soeur avait en elle une certaine nostalgie.*

In archaizing language, *soi* is sometimes employed: *l'aristocrate a apporté avec soi une touche d'impertinence* ('the aristocrat brought with himself a touch of impertinence').

*Soi* is normally used for non-specific things: *personne ne pensait a soi, on doit suivre soi-même son intuition, chaque journée amenait avec soi son lot de plaisirs partagés.*

Grevisse tells us that at the start of the 17th century *soi* began to retreat from *'lui'*, *'elle(s)'*, *'eux'*. However, *soi*, representing a subject with a determined meaning, was, in the 17th century, much more frequent than today (§640 4° Hist.).

27. There are six children in the playground.

28. I went to pay a visit to my sister.

## SOI-DISANT

*Ne compte pas sur tes soi-disant amis.*[29]

*Soi-disant* ('so-called') is invariable.

## SONGER

*Elle songe à ses enfants toute la journée.*[30]

Here, with a noun denoting a person, we should say *songer à lui, à elle*, just as we say *penser à lui, à elle*. For a thing rather than a person, we say *y songer, y penser (à cela)* : *Des vacances au mois de mai, j'y songe.*

## SONNANT ET TRÉBUCHANT

*J'exige d'être payé pour cette transaction en espèces sonnantes et trébuchantes.*[31]

Both are used as adjectives.

## SOT-L'Y-LAISSE

*Le sot-l'y-laisse est ma partie préférée du poulet.*[32]

Invariable compound noun denoting the 'oyster meat' found in two small round pieces at the rump of poultry, a piece of meat renowned for its taste. Literally, it translates as 'the fool leaves it there' / 'you'd be foolish to leave it'.

## SOUFFRIR

*Les épreuves qu'elle a souffertes* (agrees with the direct object). *Les années qu'elle a souffert* (*les années* is the circumstantial [temporal] complement, so there is no agreement).

See also COURIR.

## SOUHAITER

*Nous souhaitons remercier ce chaleureux public.*

The verb *souhaiter* is directly transitive (*souhaiter quelque chose*). It is therefore not followed by the preposition '*à*'.

Despite this, we say *nous tenons à remercier.*

29. Do not count on your so-called friends.
30. She thinks of her children all day.
31. I demand to be paid for this transaction in cold hard cash.
32. The oyster meat is my favourite part of the chicken.

## SOUPIRAIL

*La lumière passait entre deux soupiraux et éclairait la pièce.*[33]

The plural form of *soupirail* ends in *–aux*, as do the plural forms of: *bail*, *corail*, *émail*, *fermail*, *travail*, *vantail*, and *vitrail.*

## SOUSCRIRE

*Tu as souscrit à cette assurance-vie ? Oui, j'y ai souscrit.*[34]

Insurance is something to which one subscribes, and therefore, the pronoun is '*y*'. For the indirect object complement, there is a distinction between the animate and the inanimate. An insurance is not a person, and therefore not '*lui*', but '*y*', such as for example, '*j'y vais*' for a place, but '*aller à lui*' for a person.

## SOUSSIGNÉ

*Je soussigné(e) M., Mme, ou Mlle déclare…*[35]

*Soussigné* is a noun (*le soussigné* is 'the undersigned', i.e. the person who signs at the foot of the page).

## SOUVENIR (SE)

In the imperative: *souviens-t'en ; souvenons-nous-en.*

One should write:

*On se souvient de quelque chose /On se rappelle quelque chose* [and not *On se rappelle* ***de*** *quelque chose*].

*On s'en souvient /On se* ***le*** *rappelle* [and not '*on s'****en*** *rappelle*' ; even though this expression is synonymous with *se souvenir*, it cannot be used with a direct object]:

Examples:

*Elle se souvient du voyage qu'elle a fait.*
*Elle se rappelle le voyage qu'elle a fait.*
*Elle s'en souvient très bien.*
*Elle se le rappelle très bien.*

33. The light filtered through two basement windows, and illuminated the room.
34. Did you subscribe to this life insurance? Yes, I subscribed to it.
35. I, the undersigned, Mr, Mrs, or Miss [Surname] declare…

*Se rappeler de* + an infinitive is non-standard:

*Il s'est rappelé de lui avoir téléphoné.*

*De* should be avoided after *rappeler.*

One would say : *Il s'est souvenu de lui avoir téléphoné* and *Je me rappelle lui avoir dit qu'elle était belle.*

*Se souvenir* is a purely or essentially pronominal verb. The past participle agrees with the subject: *elle s'est souvenue.*

In Guillaume Apollinaire's *Le Pont Mirabeau, « il me souvient que… »* is a more literary way of saying *« je me souviens »* :

*Sous le pont Mirabeau coule la Seine*
*Et nos amours*
*Faut-il qu'il m'en souvienne…*[36]

The anaphoric pronoun *en* in *il m'en souvient* stands for *nos amours.*

See also RAPPELER (SE).

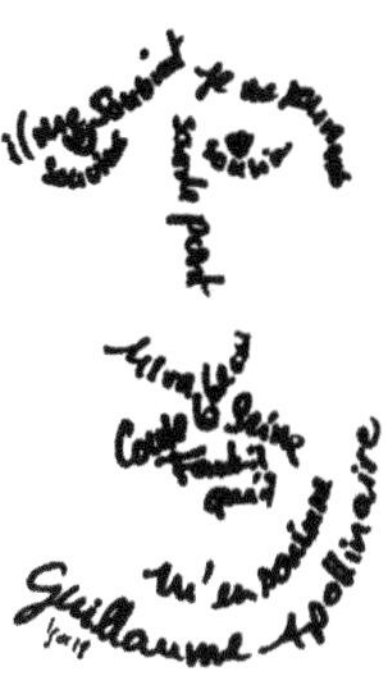


APOLLINAIRE

## STUPÉFIER

*Vous me stupéfiez par vos connaissances en mathématiques.*[37]

As with the verb *étudier*, do not forget the '*i*' in the present tense of:

*stupéfie, stupéfies, stupéfie, stupéfions, stupéfiez, stupéfient.*

## SUBJUNCTIVE (FORM OF FIRST-GROUP VERBS ENDING IN *–ER*)

The first- and second-person plural subjunctive is derived from the first-person plural indicative forms.

Starting from the root of the indicative, we add the endings *–ions* and *–iez*. For example, *oublions* minus *–ons* gives the root *oubli–*. We then add the ending *–ions*, giving the form *oubli-ions*, with double '*i*' (the final '*i*' from the root plus the '*i*' at the beginning of the ending). Similarly, adding *–iez* gives the form *oubliiez*, for the second person plural, also with double '*i*'. The pronunciation of the imperfect is the same as the indicative present with one '*i*'.

36. 'Under the Mirabeau bridge flows the Seine
And our loves // Must I remember them…'

37. Your knowledge of mathematics astounds me.

Why don't we use a *'y'* in these subjunctive forms?

—The *'y'* (which comes from Greek) replaces the ipsilon [ι] (also known as 'upsilon' [υ] through a misunderstanding by Latin speakers), the lower case form of which was written like a *'u'* [υ] and the upper case like a *'Y'* [Y]. It is used for words of Greek origin and learned forms (*psychanalyste*, *psychiatre*, *psychologue*) and also marks vowels separated by a hiatus (*ayons*, *payons*, *pays*, *paysage*), except when this hiatus is marked by an *'h'* (as in *trahi*).

Why is there no future subjunctive?

—The present tense is used for everything that is happening or may happen from the present onwards (and so covers present and future time). To stress the future, we use an adverb, a complement or a lexical expression, or simply rely on the context to make it clear:

*Je crains qu'il ne se blesse quand il ira au camp d'été.*[38]

With the subjunctive, there are only two time periods, the past and the present, necessarily oriented towards the virtual or hypothetical.

## SUBORDINATE CLAUSES OF TIME

Example 1:

*À peine terminait-elle son repas, qu'elle se mettait à lire.*[39]

The use of the pluperfect after *à peine*, as here, implies that the action is repeated or habitual. The sentence *À peine eut-elle terminé /termina-t-elle son repas, qu'elle se mit à lire*, with the past anterior or past historic, points to a single fact that happened only once.

The use of a pluperfect in a subordinate clause of time with the *passé composé* or the *plus-que parfait* is possible.

38. I am afraid that he will hurt himself when he goes to summer camp.

39. As soon as she had finished her meal, she would start reading.

EXAMPLE 2:

*Elle avait à peine terminé son repas qu'elle s'est mise à lire.*[40]
Here there is an opposition between a tense associated with the imperfect which expresses a backdrop and a punctual event in the *passé composé*. This structure is associated with spoken French. In spoken French, the inversion would not be used (*à peine avait-elle terminé*).

EXAMPLE 3:

*Elle avait à peine terminé son repas qu'elle s'était mise à lire.*[41]
This example refers back to a past within the past, which is used as a backdrop for a description.

## SUCCÉDER (SE)

*Les années se sont succédé sans que nous nous en soyons rendu compte.*[42]

This sentence means *les années ont succédé aux années*. *'Se'* is indirect: the past participle remains invariable.

## SUFFIRE (À / DE)

*Fumer, cela suffit à nous ennuyer.*

This sentence means *'quelque chose est suffisant à…'*

*Cela est assez pour nous ennuyer* = 'nothing more is needed for this outcome'.

*Cela suffit à leur faire haïr les mathématiques* = 'nothing more is needed to make them hate mathematics'.

*Il suffit de le faire pour comprendre* = 'doing it is enough to come to an understanding', 'no further explanation is needed'.

*Il suffit d'essayer* = 'simply to try is sufficient /is all that is expected /is enough.'

*Il suffit de le demander* = 'you only have to ask for it.'

*Il suffit de s'excuser* = 'nothing more, and nothing different, is expected.'

*Il suffit d'un bon pull pour ne pas souffrir du froid.*[43] = 'a good jumper is enough to be warm; there is no need for anything more.'

40. As soon as she had finished eating her meal, she started reading.
41. As soon as she had finished eating her meal, she had started reading.
42. The years passed by, without our ever even realising.
43. All you need is a good jumper to protect you from the cold.

## SUGGÉRER

*Suggérer* takes the indicative when it means *donner à penser que :*

*La recrudescence de mots anglais dans le rap français suggère qu'il a été influencé par les États-Unis.*

*Suggérer* takes the subjunctive when it means *proposer :*

*Je suggère que vous fassiez les courses.*

Under the influence of the English *to suggest*, in French *suggérer* is sometimes used instead of verbs or phrases such as *indiquer*.

## SUPPOSER QUE

When *supposer que* means 'to be led to think that', the indicative is usually used:

*Je suppose que Pierre viendra avec sa femme.*

*Je suppose que Marie a refusé ton invitation.*

When *supposer que* means 'put forward as a hypothesis that…', the subjunctive is preferable:

*Supposons que la prairie soit deux fois plus grosse qu'elle n'est.*[44]

The subjunctive is the mode of the virtual. In using the subjunctive, we question the truth of an affirmation which is unrealised, hypothetical.

## SURJONCTIF

The '*surjonctif*' is a mood imagined by Raymond Queneau, with a purely ludic and emphatic goal:

*Ah! Que ne chantassassent point les sages de l'Antiquité!*

QUENEAU

## SUSURRER

*Il lui a susurré quelques mots doux dans le creux de l'oreille.*[45]

This verb, which stems from the Latin *susurrare*, is spelled with one 's' (pronounced /s/) in the middle, and double 'r'.

44. Let us imagine that the meadow is two times larger than it actually is.

45. He whispered sweet nothings in her ear.

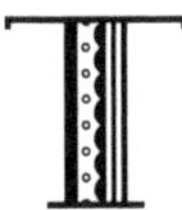

## TABLE / TABLEAU

*Tabula* is the table of the poor, made of a large wooden plank resting on supports. The *mensa* on which food was spread to be savoured while sitting on a kind of divan gave rise to the Spanish *mesa*. *Tabula*, which, at the onset, indicated in Latin a plank, gave rise to the words *table* (feminine) and *tableau* (masculine); *tabula picta* = 'painted plank'.

See MASCULINE/FEMININE.

## TANDIS QUE

*Il se plaignait tout le temps, tandis qu'elle ne bronchait pas.*[1]

Does not take the subjunctive.

*Tandis que* also readily occurs at the beginning of the sentence:

*Tandis que je lisais, ma tante devisait de tout et n'importe quoi.*[2]

Pronunciation: both pronunciations (with an audible '-*s*' and with a silent '-*s*') are acceptable: *Le Petit Robert* gives the more widespread pronunciation: tɑ̃dik(ə); *Larousse* and *Hachette* also give tɑ̃di(s)k(ə).

## TANT / TELLEMENT

*J'aime tant /tellement les poèmes de Rimbaud.*

*Tant* and *tellement* are synonyms.

*Tant* is used especially with *que* and in certain expressions:

> *Tant va la cruche à l'eau qu'à la fin elle se brise.*[3]
> *Vous m'en direz tant.*[4]

1. He complained all the time, whereas she did not bat an eyelid.
2. While I was reading, my aunt was talking about everything and nothing.
3. 'The pitcher goes to the water so often that in the end it breaks' (literal translation). Some possibilities for translating this saying are: 'If you play with fire, you end up getting burned', 'If you run too many risks, you will be in trouble', 'Don't push your luck'.
4. Tell me about it.

*Tellement* can always be used with *que* or on its own.

Etymologically *tant* means *aussi grand (que)*. Etymologically *tellement* means *de telle manière*.

Both mean *à un degré supérieur*.

In *j'aime tant les poèmes de Rimbaud*, there is a nuance of emotion on the part of the speaker, but *tant* is a little more old-fashioned and of a higher register than *tellement*. The name of an old Radio-Canada programme draws on this subtlety: *Je vous ai tant aimé !*

RIMBAUD

## TANT QUE (EN)

*Mon expérience en tant qu'enseignant de français et mon dernier travail de traducteur m'ont beaucoup apporté.*[5]

*Comme* can also be used in the sense of *en tant que* ('as') which implies 'in the capacity of': *Comme enseignant, il est assez doué*. The difference in meaning is very slight. *En tant que* is of a higher register.

## TEL / TEL QUEL

*Tel que* agrees with the preceding noun: *Des fleurs telles que la rose.*

*Tel* agrees with the following word: *Le poète telle une hirondelle.*

*Comme tel* and *en tant que tel* agree with the comparison term: *Ces légumes cuisinés comme tels* (or *en tant que tels*) *sont fades.*[6]

*Tel quel* agrees with the noun to which it relates: *Ces mots s'écrivent tels quels.*

## TEMPS (AU)

*J'ai raté sa venue et bien au temps pour moi.*[7]

*Au temps* should not be confused with its homophone *autant* (cf. *j'aime les framboises autant que les groseilles*).

5. My experience as a professor of French and as a translator has given me a great deal.
6. These vegetables, cooked like that, are bland.
7. I missed his (/her) arrival and it was my fault.

## TENIR

*Il s'en est tenu à l'essentiel.*[8]

The word *en* probably comes from the pronoun *en* (*de lui*, *d'elle*, *de cela*, etc.) and has lost this sense over time.

*Se tenir* without *en* has another meaning, as in the expression *se tenir à carreau* ('stay out of harm's way' or 'to watch one's step').

## TENSE CONCORD

Can a past anterior combine with a perfect tense (for example, *dès qu'il eut terminé…il est allé*) –?

—Normally in literary French, we would have a past historic in combination with a past anterior: « *Le verbe principal est souvent au passé simple* », but it is sometimes in another past tense (Grevisse and Goosse: 1993, 1256). They give the following example: « *Après que Jacques fut reparti, je me suis agenouillé près d'Amélie.* » (—Gide, *La Symphonie pastorale*).[9]

In spoken language, the past historic is found even less frequently than the past anterior. The past historic is reserved for the written language, and especially literary registers. Here is another example, from *Le Bon usage* (*ibid.*), this time with a pluperfect indicative: « *Après que les La Trave eurent ramené Anne vaincue à Saint-Clair, Thérèse … n'avait plus quitté Argelouse.* » (—Mauriac, *Thérèse Desqueyroux*).[10]

In standard and colloquial language, it is better to use alternative constructions: *Après avoir fini ses travaux, il est allé se reposer.*[11]

In Jean Echenoz's novel *14*, the author mixed imperfect subjunctives with compound past tenses. We even find compound past tenses with the past anterior:

« *Un éclat d'obus avait arraché tout le dessus du sac…,*

8. He stuck to the most important part.
9. Once Jacques had left again, I kneeled down beside Amélie.
10. 'After the La Trave family (/the La Traves) brought the defeated Anne back to Saint-Clair, Thérèse…had not left Argelouse anymore.'
11. He finished his work and then immediately went to rest.

*sac également percé par un projectile qu'il a retrouvé à l'intérieur après qu'il eut aussi déchiré sa veste.* »[12]

The perfect tense has taken on more and more of the functions of the past historic, hence the uses which we have noted above. These uses are typical of linguistic and grammatical change, so they cannot be ignored. This is probably more than just a question of register – it represents evolution from one form of language to another.

See also IMPERFECT SUBJUNCTIVE.

## TIC-TAC

*On entendait le tic-tac de l'horloge de grand-maman.*[13]

This onomatopoeic compound noun is invariable. Since the 1990 spelling reform, *tictac* is also acceptable.

## TITLES OF WORKS

When the headword in a title is a common noun which describes the genre of the work (*histoire*, *comédie*, *mémoires*, etc.) and is accompanied by a determiner, the verb in the surrounding sentence agrees in gender and number with that noun:

« *Les Lettres sur Jean-Jacques, composées vers 1787, sont le premier ouvrage de Mme de Staël* » (—Sainte-Beuve, *Portraits de femmes*).

*Les Confessions ont été publiées.*

*Les Pensées philosophiques servaient la cause de leur auteur.*

SAINTE-BEUVE

In other examples, those which do not include a common noun, or which do not have a determiner, usage is not fixed:

*Phèdre aura été jouée* (—Edmond de Goncourt, *La Faustin*, V): with agreement.

*Quatre femmes a été fort bien joué* : with no agreement.

For a detailed explanation, see Grevisse and Goosse (1993, 665-668). See also CAPITALS.

12. A piece of shrapnel had ripped off the entire top of the bag…, a bag that had also been pierced by a projectile which he retrieved from inside the bag, after it had also ripped his jacket.
13. We heard the tick-tock of grandmother's clock.

## TOPINAMBOUR

*Pendant la guerre, on mangeait souvent des topinambours.*[14]

The word would have been borrowed from that of a Brazilian tribe (Rey : 1998, vol. 3, 3849). Sometimes the plural *topinambaulx* is found, even if *topinambours* is the commonly accepted form.

## TOUCHER

For a living being, the verb *toucher* means to come into contact while experiencing the sensations related to touch (heat, pleasure, etc.) = to feel, to palpate, to touch a person for the pleasure of touching…
*Toucher à* is to touch but excludes the idea of the sensations of the touch, or implies harm – mostly in negative expressions, for example: *touche pas aux animaux.*

## TOUJOURS

*Elle est toujours aimable.*
*Toujours est-il qu'il avait tort.*[15]

Purists recommend no liaison with the '*-s*'. However, as Encrevé notes (1988, 47), actual usage varies.

## TOUS

The '*-s*' of the pronoun is pronounced (*Je les aime tous*), unlike the '*-s*' of the adjective (*tous les citoyens*).

## TOUT

This adverb agrees for reasons of euphony when it comes before a feminine adjective beginning with a consonant or an aspirated '*h*' : *L'actrice est toute belle* ; *cette chienne est toute hargneuse* ('aggressive'); but is invariable before a silent '*h*' or a vowel: *Elle est tout étonnée par sa réussite* ; *elle est tout heureuse.*

One would write: *Ils sont tout feu tout flamme* ;[16] *elles /ils sont tout ouïe.*

14. During the war, one often ate Jerusalem artichokes /sunchokes.
15 Nevertheless, he was wrong.
16 They are aflame with passion /all fired up.

## TRAITER

*Dans ce livre, l'auteur traite de spiritualité.*

Transitive verb with a direct object:

*Traiter quelque chose* : 'study in a profound manner' e.g. *Traiter un sujet difficile ; traiter une question épineuse.*

Particularly – to represent something, in a certain manner, in a work of art: *Chagall traitant la Bible.*

Transitive verb with an indirect object:

*Traiter de :* to have as a subject, dissertate or write about, to be on.

*Nous traiterons ici de l'immigration au cours du XXème siècle.*

## TRENTE-TROIS

When visiting a doctor in a francophone country, a patient may be asked to state repeatedly the number « *33* ». The pronunciation of *33* in French allows the doctor to hear the loud sounds emitted by the larynx through the drawing of air into the lungs and the vibrating of the rib cage.

## TURQUOISE

*Cet artiste peint ses ciels avec des bleus turquoise.*[17]

Like *topaze*, *souffre*, *grenat*, *fraise*, *nacre*, *argent*, and *kaki*, *turquoise* is a common noun used adjectivally.

It is invariable in form.

## TUTOIEMENT

In Quebec, the use of « *tu* » has spread to all levels of society over the last few decades. « *Vous* » is still used, but it is not unusual for an employee to use « *tu* » to his /her boss. A calque of the English *you*, which was originally of an informal register but which replaced the archaic form *thou*, « *tu* » is the mark of an egalitarian mindset. Using « *vous* » with someone is perceived negatively as imposing distance between speaker and hearer.

17. This artist paints his skies with turquoise blues.

Do we use « *tu* » with God?

—The biblical languages Hebrew and Greek both used the equivalent of *tu* with God. In French, *tu* is usually used in this context: *Notre Père Qui es aux cieux que Ton nom soit sanctifié…*[18] It is also usual to use *tu* for Jesus and the Virgin Mary, although *vous* persists in prayer (« *Je vous salue Marie…* »). In the *King James Bible*, the archaic form 'Thou' is used to address Jesus: 'Jesus, Thou Son of David, have mercy on me' (Luke 18:38).

**UN**

The sentence « *Il fête ses 1 an* » is erroneous.

—It should read: *Il fête son premier anniversaire,* (or, in figurative language, *…sa première année complète*).

UN

18. Our Father which art in heaven, hallowed be Thy name.

## VACANCES

*A chaque période de vacances, je me ressource à la campagne.*[1]

As the word *vacances* does not exist in the singular form with this meaning, it is not possible to say « *chaque vacances* ». In the singular, the word has a different meaning (*la vacance du pouvoir*[2]).

## VAIR / VERRE

*La pantoufle de verre de Cendrillon m'a toujours fasciné, quand j'étais petit.*[3]

In his fairy-story, Perrault wrote *verre*, but Balzac subsequently corrected what he thought to be a mistake in favour of the noun *vair*, meaning *fourrure* ('squirrel fur'). It is believed that Perrault transcribed a story he heard and consequently he confused *verre* with *vair* as they are homophones, *verre* being a much more familiar word.

PERRAULT

## VALOIR

See VIVRE.

## VA-T-EN GUERRE

*Te souviens-tu de la chanson « Malbrough s'en va-t-en guerre » ?*[4]

This expression is used either an adjective or as a noun and includes a '*-t-*' for reasons of euphony. Not to be confused with the form of the elided pronoun in the imperative used without a following hyphen: *Va-t'en.* The imperative of *aller (va)* is written without an '*–s*'.

1. Whenever holiday time comes around, the countryside gives me a new lease of life.
2. The power vacuum.
3. As a young boy, I was always fascinated by Cinderella's glass slipper.
4. Do you remember the song 'Marlborough has left for the war'?

## VAL

*Ces vals ensoleillés sont de toute beauté.*[5]

The plural is normally '*vals*'. The plural form '*vaux*' is found in rare toponymic expressions (e.g. *Les Vaux de Cernay* in the *Vallée de Chevreuse*) and in the expression « *par monts et par vaux* ».

## VAUVERT

*Il habite au diable vauvert / Vauvert.*[6]

The expression comes from *le château Vauvert* (originally *le val vert*, now in the *place du Jardin du Luxembourg*) which had a bad reputation. As a ruin, it became a refuge for thieves and other criminals and people quickly came to believe that it was haunted by the Devil.

## VÉGANE / VÉGÉTALIEN / VÉGÉTARIEN

*Il est devenu végane du jour au lendemain.*[7]

The *végétalien* does not eat any animals or animal product, including eggs, milk and honey.

The *végétarien* refuses the consumption of meat in all its forms, fish and crustaceans.

The *végan*e (the Anglicism *vegan* is less frequent in the French language) goes beyond the *végétalien* diet by excluding everything that comes from animal exploitation (wearing fur, leather, and silk for instance).

## VÉLO

*Je suis parti à vélo.*

*À vélo* is preferable to *en vélo.* The key here is whether the traveller is inside the vehicle or not.

Compare *à pied*, *à cheval*, but *en train*, *en avion*, *en voiture.*

5. These sunlit valleys are stunning.
6. He lives in the middle of nowhere.
7. He became an ethical vegan overnight.

## VELOURS

*Ils portent encore des pantalons de velours le dimanche.*[8]

The word *velours* is spelled with a single '*–s*' in French. This '*–s*' can be explained by the etymology of the word: in the Burgundy dialect *veleur*, *velor* ; in Italian *velluto* ; in Vulgar Latin *vellutum*, from which comes the verbal form *velouter*.

## VERS / ENVIRON

*Vers :* around, at (a time):

*Vers huit heures, un orage éclata.*

*On a déterminé que cette météorite a touché le sol vers les années 1600.*[9]

*Il travailla jusque vers huit heures.*

*Environ :* roughly, approximately:

*Il y avait environ 350 spectateurs.*

*Il est parti depuis environ trente minutes.*

*Les deux villages sont séparés de 20 kilomètres environ.*[10]

In fact, *vers* is a preposition and *environ* is an adverb. The structure « *il travailla jusque vers huit heures* » is an exception, because two prepositions (*jusque vers*) should theoretically not be able to follow one another. Incidentally, one could also say *Il travailla jusqu'à huit heures environ* (whereas in all other examples, *vers* and *environ* are not substitutable).

## VIEUX / VIEIL / VIELLE / VIEILLES

This adjective takes several forms:

*Une vieille femme* (feminine) /*de vieilles femmes.*

*Un vieil anarchiste* (masculine + vowel) /*de vieux anarchistes.*

*Un vieux monsieur* (masculine + consonant) /*de vieux messieurs.*

The masculine plural is always *vieux*.

8. They still wear velvet trousers on Sundays.
9. It was determined that this meteorite hit the earth around the 1600s.
10. The two villages are approximately 20 kilometres apart.

## VILLE

*Il est parti en ville.*

In general, *en ville* is more common, but dictionaries also give *aller à la ville.* Certain French-English dictionaries also give the two expressions. The expression *à la ville* tends to be used when the proper name of the city follows (*aller à la ville de Chambéry*) and also in opposition to *à la campagne* (*elle passe l'hiver à la ville*).

## VINGT

Base 20 came from the Gallic language (80 = 4 groups of 20). *Septante* comes from the Latin word *'septuaginta'* and *nonante* from *'nonaginta'* ; *octante* also exists (these numbers are base 10). These are regional variations used in Belgium, Luxembourg, and Swizerland.

See Cent, Mille, and Quatre-vingt(s).

## VIVRE

(a) When *vivre* is used in a literal sense, it is intransitive and therefore invariable:

*Les dix ans qu'elle a vécu.*

*Dix* in *les dix ans* (with the idea of duration) is not a direct object but and adverbial phrase of time.

(b) When *vivre* is used figuratively (i.e. when the nature and quality of something experienced over a certain period is contemplated rather than its duration), it is transitive and therefore variable.

*Les heures merveilleuses qu'il avait vécues.*

In *les sept vies qu'elle a vécues*, the speaker is emphasizing not the duration (she has not lived *during* seven lives) but, figuratively, the number of lives she has lived: there is therefore agreement here.

This rule applies to verbs like *coûter*, *valoir*, *vivre*, *peser*, *marcher*, *courir*...

## VOIE / VOIX

*Elle a une très jolie voix.*
*Il a trouvé sa voie.*

*La voix* : the sounds emitted by the vocal cords. Keep in mind the Latin etymology: *vox populi.*

*La voie* : the way (in both the literal and figurative senses): *la voie du devoir ; La Voie lactée.*

We write *avoir voix au chapitre.*[11]

## VOIRE

*Il avait l'air d'avoir soixante ans, voire soixante-dix ans.*[12]

The adverb takes an '*–e*' to avoid confusion with the verb *voir. Voire* originally meant *vraiment* (from the Latin *vera* meaning 'true').

## VOULOIR

(a) Present indicative: *Je veux, tu veux, il veut, nous voulons, vous voulez, ils veulent.*

(b) Present subjunctive: *que je veuille, que tu veuilles, qu'il veuille, que nous voulions. que vous vouliez, qu'ils veuillent.*

(c) Present imperative:
*Veux* comes from the present tense form *tu veux*, and is the normal form of the present imperative, though little used.
*Veuille* comes from the present subjunctive *que tu veuilles* which itself comes from the indicative *ils veulent.*

*Veuille* has a different meaning from *veux*, meaning *je te prie de vouloir, je désire que tu veuilles.* It has become a politeness formula: *Veuillez nous répondre avant la fin du mois ; Veuillez fermer la porte.*

## VRAI / VÉRIDIQUE / VÉRITABLE

The adjectives *vrai, véritable* and *véridique* express an idea of conformity to reality, to the truth. These three adjectives thus share very similar meanings, but they are not, however, interchangeable.

11. To have one's say in a matter.
12. He seemed to be sixty, even seventy years old.

*Vrai :* that which conforms to the truth /which is real, not imaginary /which is correct. –
*Ces hypothèses sont vraies.*

*Véritable :* that which is genuine, not fake.
*C'est un véritable mur en marbre.*
In some cases, *vrai* and *véritable* are practically interchangeable (*du vrai marbre /du marbre véritable* ; *c'est un vrai boute-en-train /c'est un véritable boute-en-train*[13]) – this is above all a question of register (with *véritable* being a little more elevated).

COLUCHE

*Véridique :* Suitable for a text, a testimony that is accurate, in line with reality.
*Ce témoignage est véridique.*

13. He's a true /real clown.

## WAGON

Has a nonstandard pronunciation used in the North of France, where it is pronounced with an initial [v] and not [w].

## WATTEAU

*La carrière du peintre Antoine Watteau fut brève.*[1]

The name of the painter, Watteau, is pronounced with an initial /v/ sound.

WATTEAU

## WIFI

*Nous n'avons pas de Wifi dans ce petit village rural de France.*[2]

Numerous orthographic variations exist, such as wifi, Wifi, wi-fi or Wi-Fi. The noun is masculine.

The pronunciation is [wifi] and not [waɪfaɪ].

## XYLOPHONE

*Il a appris la musique sur un xylophone.*[3]

Even if xylophone in Greek is pronounced /ksilophono/, the tendency in French is to say [gzilɔfɔn]. *Le Robert* gives the two pronunciations.

1. The painter Antoine Watteau's career was short-lived.
2. We do not have Wifi in this small rural village in France.
3. He learned to play music on a xylophone.

## Y

*Je m'y rendrai dans quelques jours.*[1]

There are situations in which we cannot use *'y'* ; for example, in *j'irai là où tu veux* [rather than *j'y irai où tu veux*]. *'Y'* is an anaphoric pronoun: from the moment that the verb is followed by a complement of place, no matter what it is, *'y'* is not needed in these contexts [i.e. not needed as follows: *j'y irai où tu veux ; j'y irai à l'école*].

– One can say simply: *j'irai où tu veux.*

## YEUSE

*Le chêne vert communément appelé l'yeuse est un arbre à feuilles persistantes.*[2]

The liaison is compulsory (*'l'yeuse'* and *not 'la yeuse'*).

French words that start with *'y'* and are not borrowed foreign words always accept elision and liaison: *les-z-yeux* [and *not* : *les // yeux*].

Borrowed foreign words, such as *'yak'* or *'yole'* (from 'yawl'), are not elided: *le yak* ; *la yole.*

## ZIGGOURAT

*La ziggourat fut bâtie au 13e siècle avant Jésus-Christ en Mésopotamie.*[3]

Feminine noun.

1. I will go back there in a few days.
2. The green oak, also called the holm oak, is a tree with evergreen leaves.
3. The ziggurat was built in the 13th century BC in Mesopotamia.

# BIBLIOGRAPHY


Abecassis M. and Block M., 2015, *French Cinema in Close-up*, Dublin: Phaeton.

Bailly A., 1901, *Dictionnaire grec-français*, Paris : Hachette.

Beaulieux C., 1927, *Histoire de l'orthographe française, tome I : La formation de l'orthographe*, Paris : Champion.

Bescherelle, 1997, *La Conjugaison pour tous*, Paris : Hatier.

Bonnard H., *Grand Larousse de la langue française* (1971-1978), Paris : Larousse.

Bouhours D., 1971, *Doutes sur la Langue Françoise Proposez à Messieurs de l'Académie Françoise par un Gentilhomme de Province*, University of Sussex, Brighton: Committee for Research in French Studies; (reprint of first edition – Paris : S. Mabre-Cramoisy, 1674).

Brunot F., 1936, *La Pensée et la langue*, Paris : Masson.

Damourette J. et Pichon E., 1911-1936, *Des mots à la pensée. Essai de grammaire de la langue français*, 7 volumes, Paris : Ed. d'Arthrey.

Dauzat A., Dubois J. and Mitterand H., 1974, *Nouveau dictionnaire étymologique et historique*, Paris : Larousse.

Dubois J., 2002, *Dictionnaire de linguistique*, Paris : Larousse.

Encrevé P., 1988, *La liaison avec et sans enchaînement. Phonologie tridimensionnelle et usages du français*, Paris : Le Seuil.

Estienne R., 1549, *Dictionnaire françois-latin*, Paris : Estienne.

Féraud J.-F., 1768, *Dictionnaire critique de la langue françoise*, Paris : chez Vincent, 2 volumes.

Foata D. et Fuchs A., 2003, *Calcul des probabilités, Cours exercices et problèmes corrigés. Licence, écoles d'ingénieurs, agrégation interne*, Paris : Dunod.

Girodet P., 2003, *Pièges et difficultés de la langue française*, Paris : Bordas.

Grevisse M. et Goosse A., 1993, *Le Bon Usage. Grammaire française*, Paris Louvain-La-Neuve : Duculot, 1997.

Imbs P., 1960, *L'emploi des temps verbaux en français moderne*. Paris : Klincksieck.

Judge A. and Healey F. G., 1985, *A Reference Grammar of Modern French*, London, Sydney, Auckland: Arnold.

Labeau E., [in preparation] *Chronicle of a Death foretold: the French Simple Past.*

Legoarant B., 1832, *Nouvelle orthologie française, ou Traité des difficultés de cette langue, des locutions vicieuses, des homonymes, homographes, paronymes, et des verbes irréguliers,* Paris : Chez Mansut fils.

*Le Grand Larousse du XXème siècle* (six volumes), 1932, Paris : Larousse.

*Le Petit Robert*, 1993, Paris : Le Robert.

Mathieu-Colas, M., 1994, *Les Mots à trait d'union. Problèmes de lexicographie informatique*, Paris : Didier-Érudition.

Ménage G., 1672, *Observations de Monsieur Menage sur la Langue Françoise*, Paris : Chez Claude Barbin.

Mourad G., 2003, « *La virgule viendrait-elle de l'écriture arabe ? Constatations sur ses origines graphique – et fonctionnelle, dans TUGboat* », 24, 3, pp.334-8.

*Nouveau Littré*, 2006, Paris : Garnier.

Palsgrave J., 1530, *Lesclarcissement de la Langue Françoyse*, London : J. Haukyns.

Partridge, E. 1970, *A Dictionary of Slang and Unconventional English*, 7th edition, London: Routledge and Kegan Paul.

Pivot B., 2006, *Les Dictées de Bernard Pivot*, Paris : Livre de Poche.

Rey A., 1998, *Dictionnaire historique de la langue française*, 3 vol., Paris : Le Petit Robert.

Riegel M., Pellat J.-C. et Rioul R., 1994, *Grammaire méthodique du français,* Paris : PUF.

Vanneste A., 2005, *Le français du XXIe siècle. Introduction à la francophonie. Eléments de phonétique, de phonologie et de morphologie,* Antwerpen – Apeldoorn : Garant.

Walter H., 1988, *Le français dans tous les sens*, Paris : Robert Laffont.

## Author

**Dr Michaël Abecassis** (DEA Grenoble, DLang St Andrews) is a Senior Instructor in French and a college lecturer at the University of Oxford. He has published widely on French linguistics and cinema. His publications include *The Representation of Parisian Speech in the Cinema of the 1930s* (Peter Lang, 2005); *Le français parlé au XXIème siècle* in two volumes (L'Harmattan, 2008), with Laure Ayosso and Élodie Vialleton; *Les Voix des Français* in two volumes (Peter Lang, 2010) and *Écarts et apports des médias francophones : Lexique et grammaire* (Peter Lang, 2013), both with Gudrun Ledegen; *French Cinema in Close-up* (Phaeton, 2015), and *An Anthology of French and Francophone Singers from A to Z* (Cambridge Scholars Publishing, 2018), both with Marcelline Block.

## Illustrator

**Igor Bratusek** was born in France and graduated at Paris Sorbonne, and is now employed at Université Paris-Dauphine. His passion for drawing and photography has motivated him to illustrate this book on the French language. He particularly likes to draw portrait caricatures and drawings with an emphasis on word plays. His writings on French cinema actors, and his portrait illustrations (along with those of Jenny Batlay), are in *French Cinema in Close-up* (Phaeton, 2015), and in *An Anthology of French and Francophone Singers from A to Z* (Cambridge Scholars Publishing, 2018).

Lightning Source UK Ltd.
Milton Keynes UK
UKHW021810140419
340994UK00005B/185/P